First M.E. Church.
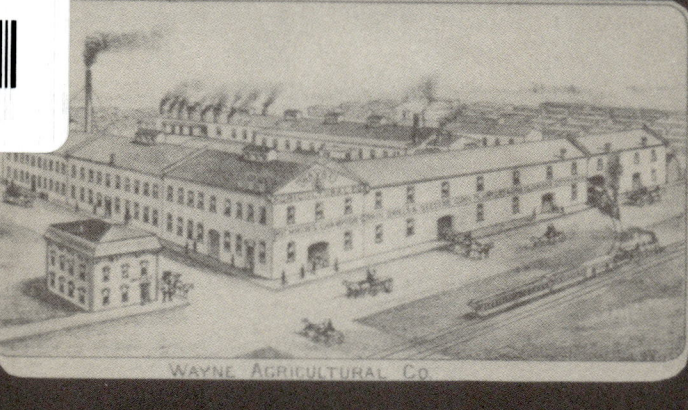
Wayne Agricultural Co.

Chase Piano Factory.

Zeller & Co. Cracker Manufactory.

White Water Tannery.

Richmond Gas Works.

First National Bank.

Geo. H. Knollenberg.

Empire Steel Plow Works.

Matthews, Winder & Co.

W.C. Starr & Son.

Irvin Reed & Sons.

Grand Opera House.

Sedgwick Brothers.

On behalf of the Board of Directors, officers and employees of Star Bank, we are pleased to present ***Richmond: A Pictorial History***. We extend our sincere thanks to the authors and to the many people whose photographs, memories and knowledge of local history helped to make this book possible.

Star Bank is proud to have played a prominent role in the city's development for 122 years. It is with special pride that we bring you this handsome volume. We hope it will be a valuable addition to your family library and a collector's item in the years to come.

We dedicate this book to the people of Richmond, past and present, whose faith, courage and determination established the foundation for our city's growth and progress.

David W. Stidham
President
Star Bank
Richmond, Indiana

David W. Stidham

Gregory W. Edwards
Chairman
Star Bank
Richmond, Indiana

Gregory W. Edwards

Excerpts from "The Hoosier's Nest" a poem by Richmond author, John Finley

*Blest Indiana! In whose soil
Men seek the sure rewards of toil,
And honest poverty and worth
Find here the best retreat on earth
While hosts of Preachers, Doctors, Lawyers,
All independent as wood-sawyers,
With men of every hue and fashion,
Flock to this rising "Hoosher" nation.
Men who can legislate or plow
Wage politics or milk a cow–
So plastic are their various parts,
Within the circle of their arts
With equal tact the "Hoosher" loons,
Hunt offices or hunt raccoons.*

*Suppose in riding somewhere West
A stranger found a "Hoosher's" nest
In other words, a buckeye cabin
Just big enough to hold Queen Mab in
It situation low but airy
Was on the borders of a prairie,
And fearing he might be benighted
He hailed the house and then alighted
The "Hoosher" met him at the door
Their salutations soon were o'er;
He took the stranger's horse aside
And to a sturdy sapling tied;
Then, having stripped the saddle off,
He fed him in a sugar trough.
The stranger stooped to enter in,
The entrance closing with a pin,
And manifested strong desire
To seat him by the log heap fire,
Where half a dozen Hoosheroons,
With mush and milk, tincups and spoons.*

Richmond
Indiana
A Pictorial History

by Gertrude Luckhardt Ward

G. Bradley Publishing, Inc.
St. Louis, Missouri 63131

Richmond
A Pictorial History

by
Gertrude Luckhardt Ward

A limited edition of 3,000
of which this is...

370

PUBLICATION STAFF:
Author: Gertrude Luckhardt Ward
Advisors: Myra J. Coate
          James P. Hartig
          Jean Prichard
          Dick Reynolds
Cover Artist: David Marsee
Book Design: Diane Kramer
Proof Editor: Gloria Baraks
Publisher: G. Bradley Publishing, Inc.
Sponsor: Star Bank

Known as a man who loved plants, John J. Conley (1812-1907) died at the age of 95. He was born south of Richmond, near Boston, and worked as a carpenter, joiner and cabinetmaker until 1841 when he moved to Richmond. He owned a shoe-peg factory near the Whitewater River.

He focused his interest in plants into operating his Richmond Nursery at the southeast corner of South 5th and E streets, selling trees, shrubs and flowers. He sold the nursery to Edward Y. Teas and returned to the family farm. Teas renamed the property the Cascade Nursery for the brook that flowed through it. Conley died at the home of a daughter, Lillie C. Pease of Shipley, Florida. He was the last surviving member of the Wayne County Horticultural Society and a life member of the Indiana Horticultural Society.

© Copyright 1994 by G. Bradley Publishing, Inc. All rights reserved. Printed in the United States of America. No part of this publication may be reproduced, stored in a retrieval system, or transmitted, in any form or by any means, electronic, mechanical, photocopying, recording, or otherwise without the prior permission of the publisher.

ISBN-0-949363-42-7
PRINTED IN THE UNITED STATES OF AMERICA

Table of Contents

Foreword 7

Chapter 1: In The Beginning 8

Chapter 2: Early Transportation 19

Chapter 3: Business in Richmond 40

Chapter 4: Good Times in Richmond 88

Chapter 5: Governing Richmond 126

Chapter 6: Family Life in Richmond 156

Acknowledgements 196

Contributors 197

Index 198

Holthouse and Grave Grocers shared quarters with Charles Geier Meats on 713 Main Street in this turn-of-the century picture. Notice the side of meat hanging on the right.

This photo was taken on a cobblestone Richmond street on July 3, 1882. The occasion was the departure of the Richmond LIght Infantry for an Indianapolis drill competition. The infantry was the first military brigade organized after the Civil War.

Foreword

Settled in 1806, Richmond is one of the older cities in Indiana, but surprisingly little history has been written about its rich past. This new publication is a welcome addition to the field and fills many voids left by previous works.

National land policies determined Richmond's early growth. The Northwest Ordinances of 1785-87 forbade slavery and encouraged education. A few years later in the Greenville Treaty of 1795, General Anthony Wayne took possession of land claimed by twelve Indian tribes and opened the area for development.

North Carolina Quakers such as Jeremiah Cox, John Smith and David Hoover were the first to settle on the banks of the Whitewater River. Farms flourished, mills tapped the power of the river, and by 1820 the town made its first appearance in the Federal Census with 320 people. The beginnings of Earlham College in 1847 showed the continuing Quaker influence.

Poor roads and un-navigable waterways slowed Richmond's growth until the 1830s. Then the National Road, surveyed through Richmond in 1827 and constructed soon thereafter, became the nation's east-west main street. In 1836 the *Palladium* marvelled at the subsequent wave of immigrants: "And still they come - the never-ending tide rolls on."

Some German craftsmen who helped construct the bridge over the Whitewater gorge found Richmond a hospitable place and stayed. By 1900 roughly 30% of the population claimed German ancestry, and this ethnic legacy can still be read in the names of such significant buildings as Bartel's and Knollenberg's. Later waves of migration followed and Italians, Greeks and Filipinos added to Richmond's cultural pluralism.

The legendary Underground Railroad added more diversity to Richmond as escaping southern slaves passed through seeking freedom in Canada. Many stayed, and by 1850, Wayne County had the largest black population of any county in Indiana, earning it the nickname of "Little Africa." This growing minority population attracted William P. Quinn and James Townsend to the city where they prospered as religious and political leaders.

Railroads linked Richmond to outside markets in 1853 and accelerated its growth. Early industries such as the Robinson foundry and the Gaar-Scott steam engine works now found national and international customers for their agricultural implements. New banks and a public library were symbols of Richmond's emergence as a hub, and it became the political center as well. In 1873 the county seat moved from Centerville, and in 1893 occupied the imposing new Courthouse.

The late 19th and early 20th centuries saw Richmond grow steadily in size and accomplishment. Starr pianos, McGuire lawn mowers, Gennett recordings, Hill roses, a variety of caskets and 14 different automobiles found world markets. The Richmond Art Association began in 1898 and its attachment to the high school created a relationship unique in the nation. Several local industries converted to military production in 1917 for the World War, and again in World War II, supplying goods from airplane wings to underwear. A new airport south of town was part of the defense effort in the 1940s. In the shadow of the second war, an Austrian-Jewish refugee, Norbert Silbiger, arrived and soon became the first director of Richmond Civic Theatre.

In the decades since 1945, Richmond's cultural diversity expanded as its population and economic base declined. Indiana University East and Indiana Vocational Technical College both opened new educational opportunities and enhanced the growth of the northern edge of town. The Earlham School of Religion and Bethany Seminary added graduate degrees and new activity to the west side. The Richmond Symphony and the Whitewater Opera enriched the quality of life and both found a home in the renovated Civic Hall in 1993. Although the departure of International Harvester in the 1950s and Avco in the 1970s damaged the economy, Richmond attracted Sanyo and Hill's Pet Products in the 1980s. The local population peaked in 1960 at nearly 45,000, and slowly fell to 38,000 in 1990.

National retailers lured customers away from downtown in the 1960s to shopping centers on the east and west sides of the city, and the completion of Interstate 70 drew other businesses away from the city's core to its fringes. The tragic explosion and fire of 1968 took 41 lives and did $15 million damage to the Main Street area. Richmond responded creatively to these challenges and transformed the downtown to a pedestrian promenade with an Elder-Beerman department store as retail anchor.

Richmond today, like most midwestern cities, is interdependent with global forces. The local newspaper is now a part of the national Gannett group; the two largest banks have corporate headquarters in Ohio and manufacturers such as Alcoa, Dana, Kemper, and Primex are parts of larger enterprises. Students and faculty come from around the world to Earlham, Indiana University East and Bethany. Richmond's radio stations carry nationally syndicated programs, and local citizens travel daily from airports in Dayton, Cincinnati and Indianapolis.

In the 1990s with an increasingly homogenized culture, one of Richmond's distinctions is its past. This book is a good example of pride in a unique heritage and a desire to preserve the memory of it. Both pictures and narrative recall what was special about yesterday. The author now joins in the ranks of Dalbey, Fox, Jones and Beisner who earlier contributed their interpretations of local history.

George T. Blakey
Professor of History
Indiana University East

Chapter 1:

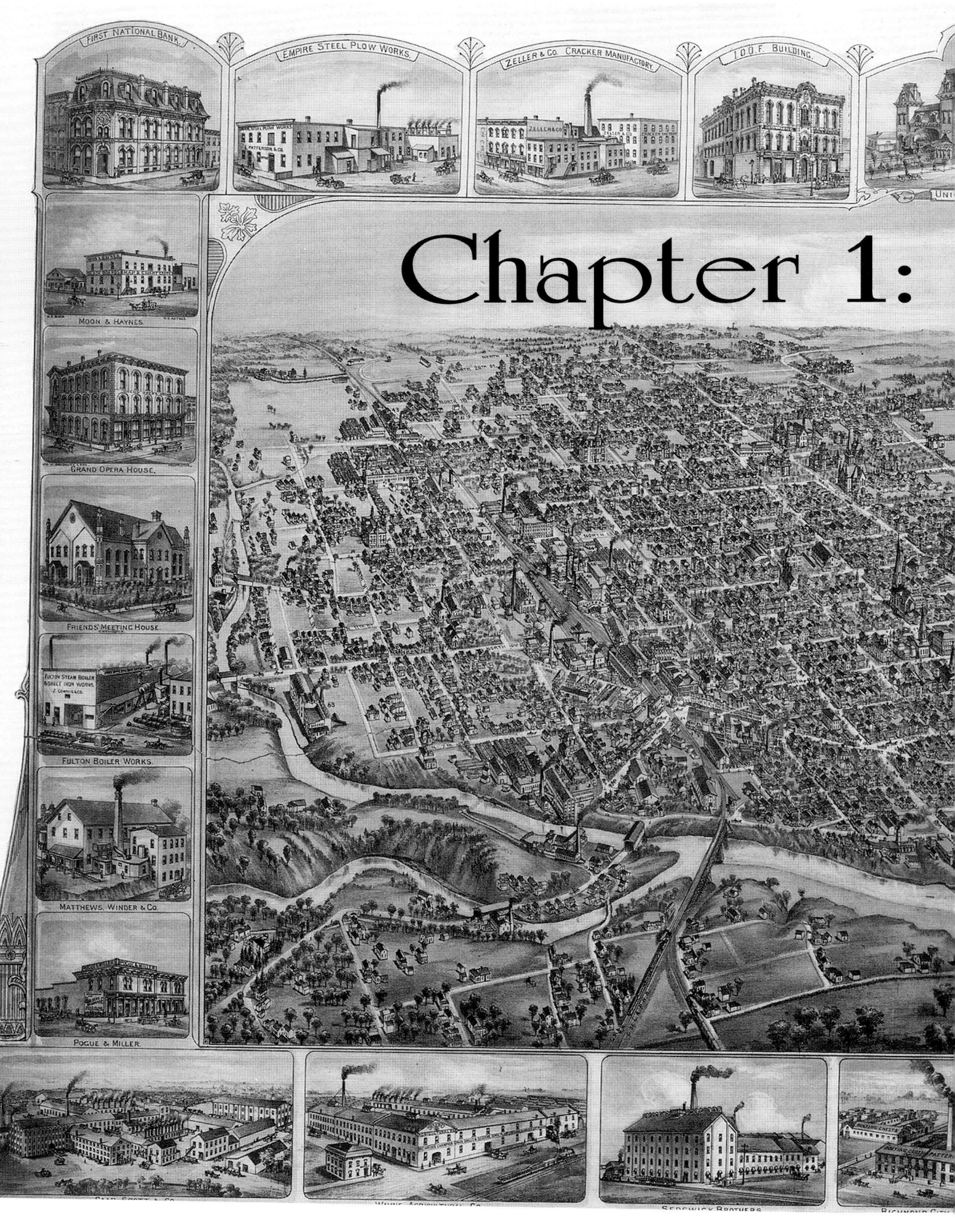

In The Beginning

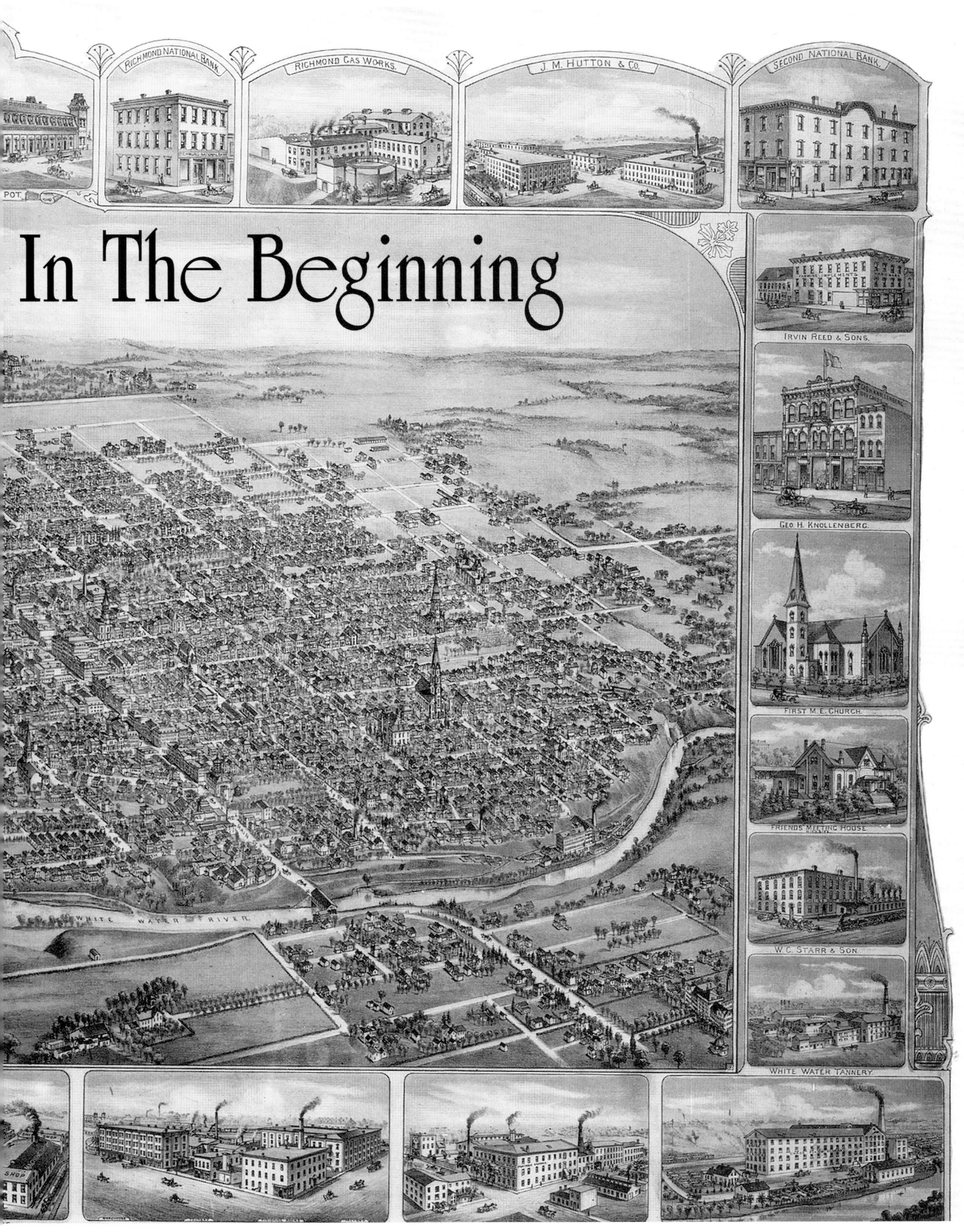

How far back does one go to determine the beginning of the city of Richmond? One starting point is the time of the great inland sea that covered this area. It was the animals, plants, microorganisms and calcium carbonate of that slightly salty sea that accumulated in layers along with some silty runoff that formed our bedrock with its array of corals, sea lilies, brachiopods, bryozoans, mollusks and trilobites. At many museums these specimens are kept in protected cases yet Richmond has enough supply that they have formed stepping stones, foundations and basement walls of many buildings. In more recent years the glaciers of ice moved south from their origins in the north and brought to Wayne County and most of northern Indiana layers of soil plus some granite rock scrubbed from what is now Canada and Michigan. It is this soil that grows our corn, soybeans, wheat and hay, and, if we are not careful of this heritage, flows south with flood waters to the Ohio and Mississippi rivers. As these huge walls of ice melted, the run-off water wore paths into the gravel and soil, becoming our rivers and streams. One stream even eroded enough gravel to form our deep Whitewater Gorge. We know relatively little about the first people who came to this part of the state, but we occasionally find evidence of their presence in the mounds that they built, often as astronomical markers or burial sites. These were the Hopewell, Woodland and Adena cultures. The question of whether or not they gave rise to the later tribes of Indians, the ones the settlers encountered, has not been satisfactorily answered. Some researchers believe that the mounds were attempts to create with soil what these people remembered from a time when they or their ancestors lived in what is now Mexico or Central America where they built mounds of stone. Constantine Rafinesque, a naturalist from Sicily who was in this country in the early 1800s, translated the history of the Delaware or Lenni Lenape Indians that had been recorded on wooden slats called the Walum Olum or Red Score. That indicated an origin in Asia with people coming across the Bering Straits and flowing eastward until they reached the Atlantic Ocean. Finding that barrier, they gradually moved back to the south and west. Perhaps there were two or more major waves of early Asiatic people who came eastward. More archaeological finds may help us learn additional pieces of this puzzle. According to the reports of early settlers the historic Indian tribes shared the area of Wayne County as a hunting and fishing preserve and not as a dwelling place.

Archeologists still find spear points, mortars and pestles from their camp sites. Wild animals, plants and humans share a propensity for going into new territory, for extending their ranges. When the Revolutionary War was over many of the soldiers and their families with them, migrated to the west. Most were seeking places to start new farms away from crowded conditions in their home states along the East Coast. Many Richmond residents have ancestors who even crossed the Atlantic or Pacific oceans to find better living conditions. There were pioneers in many decades. The French traders, the *coureurs de bois*,

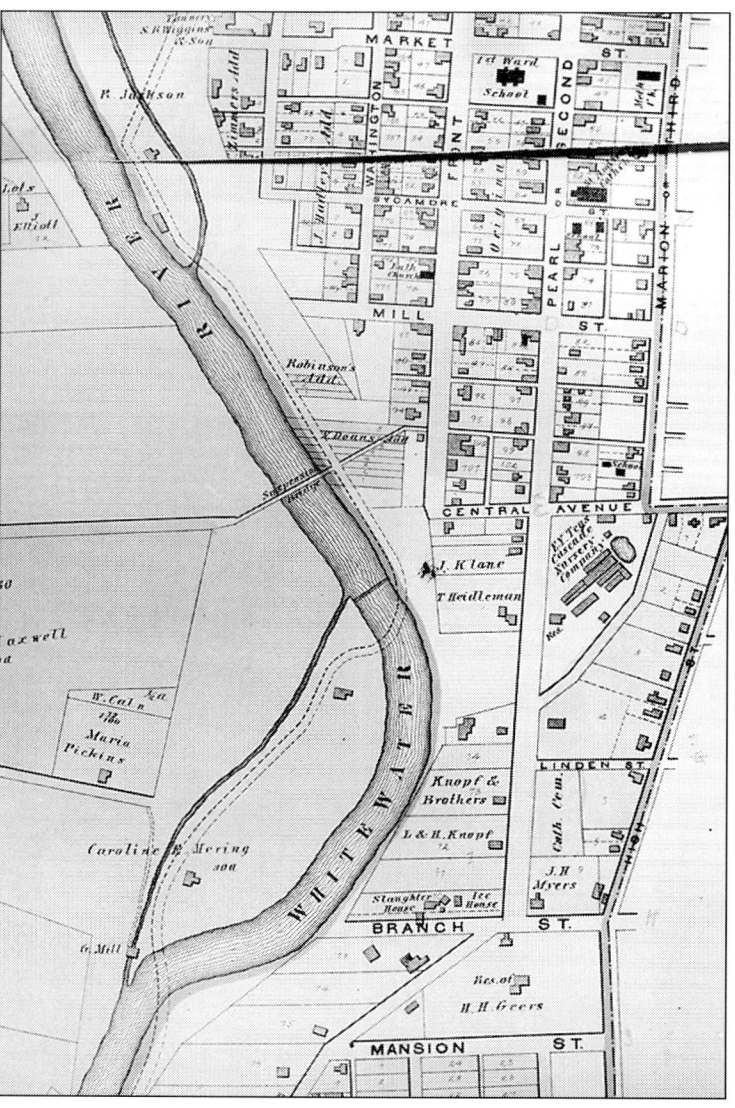

The plat surveyed by David Hoover for John Smith, one of Richmond's founders, was the basis for the north-south orientation of the city along Front, later named Fourth Street. This arrangement provided access to the mills, tannery, shoe peg factory and other work places along the Whitewater River.

were among the early travelers through the western areas, usually following the rivers and large streams where they set their traps or traded with Indians for animal skins. The furs were then taken to established trading posts. When the Northwest Territory was ceded to the United States by England in 1783 there was great hope for western expansion. Then the Northwest Ordinances of 1784, 1785 and 1787 ensured that slavery would not be allowed, that surveying would be accomplished and that schools would be supported by the income from the 640 acres of Section 16 (one of 36 sections that make up a congressional township). The surveying of the Greenville Treaty line after the peace treaty of 1795 was a major move toward settlement of what would be Richmond. The marker that shows where this line crosses the National Road stands at what is in 1994 the location of the K-Mart store near Salisbury Road. The surveyors of the Treaty line, Israel Ludlow and his crew, were among the early white men to visit this area. By

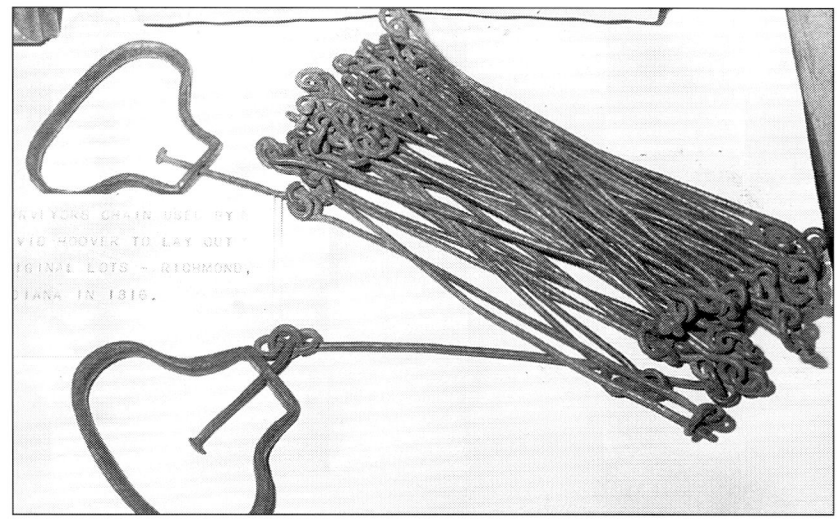

In 1816 David Hoover used his surveyor's chain, 32 feet or two rods long, to lay out lots for John Smith on his farm land, approximately along South Front and Pearl streets, bounded at the north with a fence line at Main Street. Pearl Street was later named Fifth Street.

In 1806, David Hoover, a trained surveyor, used his large Atkinson & Burke compass from North Carolina to lead four friends from their settlement at West Milton, Ohio, westward across the state line to the Middle Fork of the Whitewater River. The compass was protected in a pine box shaped to fit the valuable instrument.

David Hoover

Catherine Yount Hoover

The first home of David and Catherine Yount Hoover was a house of large squared logs near the Middle Fork of the Whitewater River, now located on Sylvan Nook Drive, built in 1807. In 1830 a brick addition in the then-current Federal style was made to the west facade of the house. This was a fitting structure for the man who served the community as a justice of the peace in 1810, associate judge of Wayne Circuit court in 1815, and clerk of the court from 1817 to 1830.

1811 there had been additional negotiations with the Indians extending government land by 12 miles, along a line parallel with the former treaty line. The marker for this line stands at the west edge of Cambridge City. Richmond's settlers arrived from at least two directions, south and east. A group called "the Kentuckians" came up the Miami River from the Ohio, and then overland to the Whitewater. Several settled in the vicinity of Short Creek. Word seemed to have reached investors and land speculators fairly early because Joseph Wasson, Peter Fleming, John Meek and Joseph Woodkirk sold some of their land to early settlers. Families of George Holman, Richard Rue and Thomas McCoy formed part of this southern group. Coming from the east were members of the Hoover family including David Hoover and his brother-in-law, William Bulla. The Hoover family originated in Switzerland where the name was spelled Huber. When they immigrated to the United States an early deed writer spelled their name as Hoover. Some members of the family migrated to near West Milton, Ohio where David's father purchased a parcel of land. The family was disappointed by the fevers that seemed to plague them so David and "four friends" set out in the spring of 1806 to travel to the newly opened land in the Indiana Territory, in what was then Dearborn County. David, 25 years of age, was a trained surveyor so he served as the "pilot" of the expedition. They were pleased to find abundant water with potential for mills, limestone for building and fertile floodplains. When they reached the Whitewater River they found an Indian campsite and learned that white settlers were located to the south. The Hoover party walked down and met Holman, Rue and McCoy before turning east for their return trip to Ohio. Their enthusiasm for what they termed their

A pageant at Earlham in 1946 included an old wagon that marked 100 years of Indiana statehood and commemorated the arduous travel by early settlers in their Conestoga wagons drawn by a team of oxen. The Studebaker family of Pennsylvania gained fame by making this sort of wagon, modeled after farm wagons of southwestern Germany. Local wagonmakers included Adam Boyd, Nathan Hawkins, Charles and David Knollenberg, John McClelland and Henry Schute.

The design of this wagon is credited to Nathan Hawkins (1782-1867), probably of New Garden Monthly Meeting near Fountain City (a Quaker settlement). Nathan was a name given to the boys in several branches of this Quaker family from South Carolina. The Hawkins family moved closer into Richmond in 1812 for protection against the Indians.

"land of Canaan" was quickly transferred to friends and relatives not only in Ohio but even back to the Carolinas where many other members of the Society of Friends, also known as Quakers were located. Those people with strong anti-slavery sentiments must have formed a minor land rush because there was a great influx of Friends coming into the Richmond area. Much of the entry was on foot, with pioneers hacking their way through the dense woody growth of trees and shrubs. When members of the Hoover family returned to the Whitewater area to make a clearing their first crop was turnips, left to grow while the men returned to prepare their families for their move. The log house with squared hewn logs still stands as part of a dwelling east of Route 27. This home dates back to 1806. In 1830 David and Catherine, his wife, added a brick house to the west side of the log house. Other changes have been made, but the log section, protected by clapboards, is the same configuration.

Mills were essential to the survival of Richmond's early settlers. In 1853 David S. Burson and Isaac P. Evans built a wooden mill (right) near the Middle Fork of the Whitewater on the road leading to Chester and south of the present Reid Memorial Hospital. The mill was designed to press valuable oil from the linseed or flax seed grown by the local farmers. Earlier mills were built for more mundane purposes such as cracking corn or sawing logs. When the frame mill burned in 1864, a brick mill was erected.

Another local crop was tobacco, requiring hand labor in planting, stripping, hanging to cure and packing for shipment to a sales barn. At one time the mill was used for stripping the leaves from the coarse stalks and drying them.

During World War I the brick building served as a training center for Army mechanics. Barracks were provided for housing the men. The brick portion was used in the 1920s for a few years by William Bockhoff and his H-K Toy and Skate Company. Local residents remember skates with wooden rollers for use in the popular indoor rinks and with steel bands for use on streets and side walks. The building was demolished in 1967 by Drs. John Mader and John Stepleton.

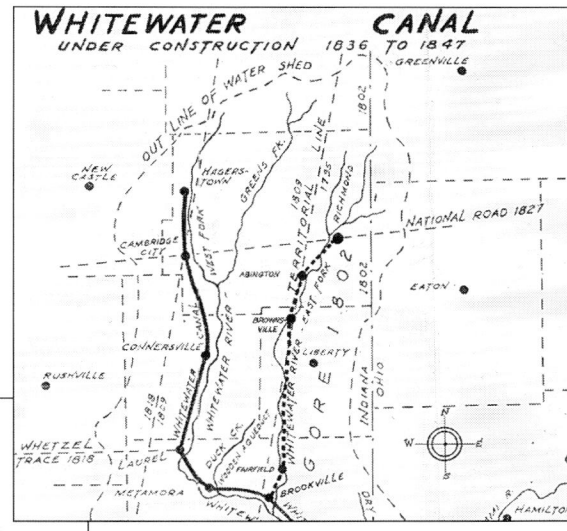

Luther Feeger, historian and former managing editor of the *Palladium-Item and Sun-Telegram*, examines the site of the proposed Richmond to Brookville Canal of 1838. This was intended to follow the bed of the East Fork of the Whitewater River to the junction with the West Fork, a distance of about 34 miles. Flooding in January 1847 caused collapse of walls on the main canal from Lawrenceburg to Hagerstown and damaged the locks so badly that the project was abandoned. This site is on old Route 27 south of Backmeyer's hill on the Liberty Pike.

The Greenville Treaty

Although the Greenville Treaty of 1795 was intended to bring peace between the twelve Indian tribes who had signed it following Gen. Anthony Wayne's successful battle at the Maumee River August 2, 1794, there was dissatisfaction among the Indians. Some historians believe that the British were instigators of the unrest. An Indian leader and Shawnee chief, Tecumseh, and his brother, The

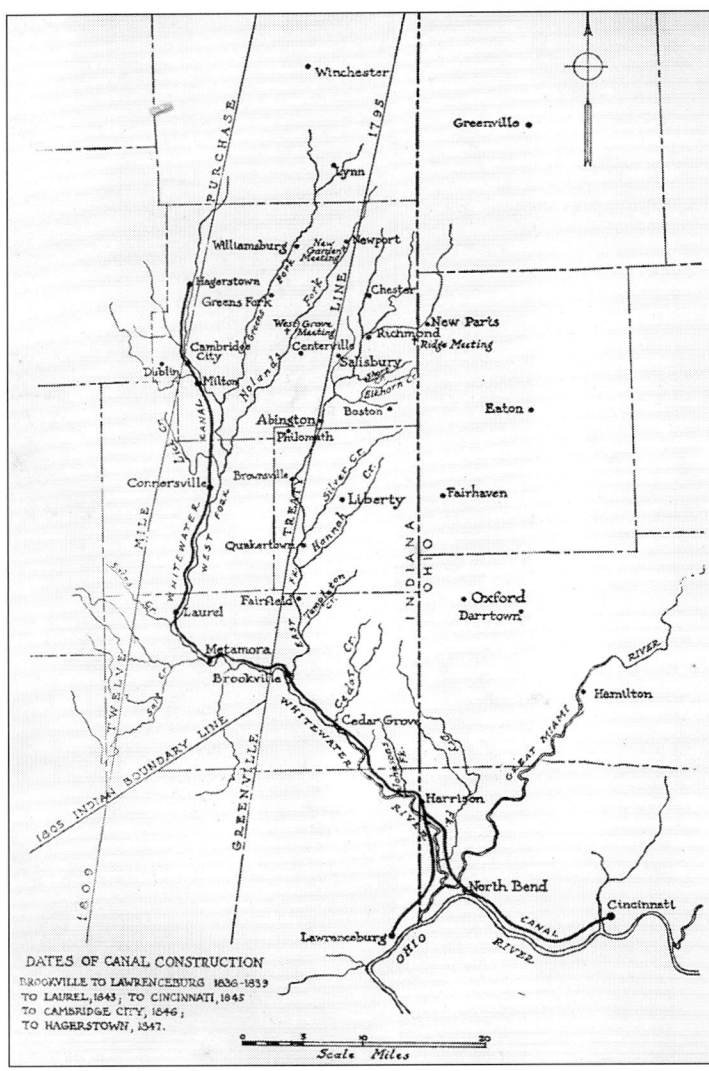

When the Treaty of Greenville was signed on August 3, 1795, and the slightly slanted line drawn from Fort Recovery to the Ohio River, the Miamis, the Weas, the Piankeshaws and the other tribes doubtless recognized that this spelled disaster for their way of life. The treaty allowed the white settlers to purchase land in Indian hunting and fishing preserves. The stone marker is found on National Road West, near its junction with Salisbury Road.

Major General Anthony Wayne (1745-1796) was chosen from 19 applicants for the task of ending the Indian fighting in the Northwest Territory. The decision came after the massacre of troops under Governor Arthur St. Clair on November 4, 1791 north of Greenville, Ohio. President George Washington had great faith in Wayne's abilities from his conduct during the Revolutionary War.

Wayne trained his recruits well with musket and bayonet for a year and was ready to move them into action by October 1793. They built Fort Recovery at the site of the St. Clair Massacre. On August 20, 1794, Wayne and his men attacked the Indians at the Battle of Fallen Timbers, winning decisively and breaking the Indian confederation.

The Indians were called to meet with Wayne at Greenville in June, 1795. More than 1,000 chiefs from nine tribes accepted the invitation, including Little Turtle, principal chief of the Miamis.

Prophet, with their braves, continued to harass the settlers east of the Greenville Treaty line. Some settlers took refuge in small forts and blockhouses.

By 1801 General William Henry Harrison had been appointed governor of the Indiana Territory with its capital at Vincennes. From 1802 to 1805 Harrison negotiated seven treaties with 10 different tribes and acquired additional territory.

This tablet marks the boundary between the government and Indian lands fixed by General Wayne and the twelve tribes signing the 1795 Greenville Treaty. It also marks the site of the county's first county seat, Salisbury as well as the birthplace of Oliver Morton, Indiana's Civil War governor. The marker was placed by the Daughters of the American Revolution in 1924.

Tecumseh and his twin brother, The Prophet or Loud Voice, were members of the Shawnee tribe, and Tecumseh had fought at the Battle of Fallen Timbers. The Prophet worked tirelessly to prevent the Delaware Indians from accepting the teachings of Moravian missionaries on the White River near Anderson. He and his band destroyed the mission in 1806. The two brothers established their own village, Prophetstown, on the Wabash River near the Tippecanoe River.

William Henry Harrison, governor of Indiana Territory, alarmed by the Indian activities, fought them at the Battle of Tippecanoe on November 7, 1811, and destroyed Prophetstown.

Early Founders

Early founders, David Hoover, John Smith and Jeremiah Cox, were leading members of the Quakers from the Carolinas who founded Richmond. John Finley, mayor of Richmond from 1852 to 1866, wrote a poem called, "The Hoosier's Nest" in 1833. It was published in the *Indianapolis Journal* and used the term "Hoosier" in print for the first time. Marcus Mote, a noted Richmond artist, painted a view of a log dwelling that was inspired by Finley's poem.

David P. Holloway (1809-1883) exemplifies those versatile early settlers who were interested in their city, their state and their country. A birthright Quaker, he was born at Waynesville, Ohio. The family moved to Cincinnati when David was four years old and then to a farm in Wayne County in 1823. David learned the printing business as an apprentice with Edward S. Buxton, publisher of the *Public Leger*. He became editor of the *Palladium* in 1833, two years after its founding by Nelson Boon. Holloway had completed his apprenticeship at the *Cincinnati Gazette.* He remained with the *Palladium* for more than 30 years.

He was elected a state representative in 1834 and state senator in 1835. President Tyler appointed him examiner of land offices. He was elected to Congress in 1854, and was appointed commissioner of patents in 1861 until his resignation in 1865. He was married to Jane Ann Paulson in 1834. His interest in farming, perhaps going back to his boyhood, is indicated by his service as first president of the Wayne County Agricultural Society.

Daniel Reid (1799-1873) was one of many Richmond settlers born in Virginia. He married Letitia Scott and in 1821 they came north to near New Paris, Ohio, where Daniel taught school for two years. In 1823 they moved a few miles west to Richmond where Daniel clerked in James McGuire's dry goods business, then worked for Robert Morrisson. A few years later he formed a partnership with Joseph P. Strattan.

In 1829 Daniel followed Morrisson as the second postmaster for Richmond, serving until 1836. President VanBuren, in 1838, selected Reid as registrar for the U.S. land office at Fort Wayne during the digging of the Wabash and Erie Canal. Daniel and Letitia had seven children before her death in Fort Wayne in 1853. Daniel resumed his friendship with Ann Gray Dougan of Niles, Michigan, a widow, native of Virginia, and a former resident of Richmond. Her father, Isaac Gray, ran a dry goods store on Main Street from 1827 to 1829. Daniel and Ann were married in 1856 and they had two children, Daniel Gray Reid and Emma Virginia Reid.

Matthew Rattray (1796-1872), a native of Paisley, Scotland, learned weaving in his home country before coming to Richmond in 1822. Once here, he set up his loom in a log house on South 4th Street.

At first he wove blankets, cloth and carpets, but by 1841 he advertised his purchase of a "Jacquard Machine" capable of weaving the new style double coverlets. Although Rattray was one of 16 weavers in Wayne County, he possessed enough public relations skill to keep his customers coming back with their skeins and balls of yarn to frequent his shop.

Rattray married Elizabeth Cheesman of Centerville, daughter of a Revolutionary War veteran. Matthew and Elizabeth's daughter, Hannah, was married in 1848 to John Milton Gaar, president of Gaar, Scott & Co., president of Second National Bank, president of F&N Lawn Mower Company, and president of the Richmond Natural Gas Co. Hannah died in 1849, and John Milton married her sister, Helen, in 1865.

Jeremiah Cox, Jr., son of Richmond founder, Jeremiah Cox, Sr.

John Smith (c. 1756-1838), a native of North Carolina, is credited with having the vision to foresee that local lands would one day furnish a good foundation for a thriving community. Smith convinced Jeremiah Cox, Sr., to join him in laying out the lots for a town despite Cox's protest that "he would rather see a buck's tail than a tavern sign." (Often one of the first buildings raised in a town was a tavern.) David Hoover laid out Smith's land in 1816 south of Main Street and Cox's, north, in 1818. Smithville and Plainfield were two names promoted for the growing community, but David Hoover mediated by suggesting the name Richmond, perhaps recalling a former abode, Richmond, Virginia.

Smith married Letitia Trueblood and they had five sons and six daughters. The family formed part of the early Quaker group which came to Wayne County in 1806. Smith's trading post, a log building, was in the area of South B and Third streets in 1810. In 1811 he raised the first brick house in Richmond. Letitia died in 1813, and circa 1818 John married Mrs. Jane Pleas of Ohio. Their only child, a daughter named Esther married Jeremiah Hadley and the couple inherited the brick house.

A large statue of a pioneer mother with two children greets a visitor to Glen Miller Park at the 22nd Street entrance. The statue is named the *Madonna of the Trail*, one of 12 placed along the National Road from Maryland to California during 1928-29 by the Daughters of the American Revolution. Richmond's statue was dedicated October 28, 1929, and was cleaned and rededicated in 1988. Sculptor August Leimbach of St. Louis carved the statue from algonite, a poured material made from crushed granite. At the 1929 dedication Harry S. Truman, then a Missouri judge, gave the main address, Fred Gennett, Jr., the flag salute and William Dudley Foulke read from his poems. Mrs. Fred Gennett presided as regent of the Richmond Chapter of the DAR.

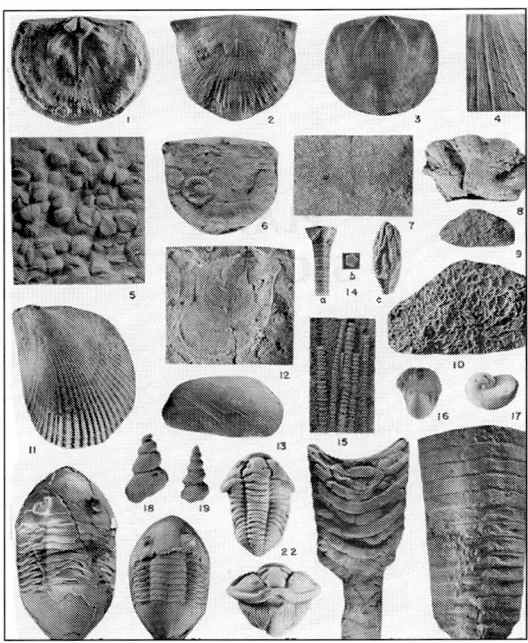

Photos or drawings of fossils from the Ordovician rocks in the Richmond formation. It was animal and plants and calcium carbonate and the slightly salty water once covering Richmond that combined and accumulated in layers to form the local bedrock. Many museums keep these pieces in cases but in Richmond they have formed stepping stones, foundations and basement walls.

Wayne County had a silver mine, but did it have silver?

In 1896 an itinerant ore finder named MacDougal came through this area with his divining rod claiming that his magic rod could find minerals underground.

His local find was at the Henry Pardieck farm south of the city near Lick Creek, now the Stonehenge gravel pit. The elder Pardiecks were not interested in digging 40 or 50 feet into the hillside on MacDougal's recommendation.

They did agree, however, to allow a Richmond company of three men, Webster Parry, Stephen Stratton and Dr. Isaac Harold, to finance the project. Several of the younger Pardiecks, including Frank, Joe, Harmon and Harry, were enthusiastic about helping dig.

A shaft went back about 60 feet into the hillside, but no visible silver was found. MacDougal's excuse was that they had gone past the lode, so he advised digging a vertical tunnel. It was sunk to 165 feet, and some mineral matter was seen, but it was reported to assay at only $8.00 per ton, not enough to justify further work.

"The Hoosier's Nest" was painted by Marcus Mote, local Quaker artist sometime between 1833 and 1860, according to Opal Thornburg, Earlham archivist. The painting illustrated a poem by Richmond author, John Finley, also managing editor of the Richmond *Palladium* and mayor of the city from 1852 until his death in 1866. The event marked Indiana history as the first reference to the name "Hoosier."

Chapter 2: Early Transportation

Early morning at 8th and Main streets, May, 1936.

Transportation on foot was the first method of getting to and around the Whitewater Valley. Most often what the pioneer carried besides himself was his food. Travel by foot was often the only option because initially there were no trails or pathways marked out for a horse or team of oxen. As the traveler moved through the maples, beeches and tulip poplars he did not see much undergrowth such as spicebush or redbud, but shrubs grew abundantly where trees had blown down or died, stinging nettles also edged the streams, and grasses grew higher than a horse.

The next progression was to use hardy ponies to carry burdens. Two men could manage a string of ponies with a large load of trade items or the pelts that were gained. Overnight the ponies would be hobbled and could crop the wild grasses or feed on the grain supply they bore.

To transport their families and possessions, most pioneers purchased a capacious wagon of German design, plus a hitch of horses, mules or oxen. Each type of animal had its defenders, some liking the speed and agility of horses or mules, others preferring the slow but steady gait of the oxen. The animals and wagons proved useful on the farms or could be sold by the settler who decided to live in town.

As the town grew, townspeople demanded lighter weight fancier carriages, sport buggies and roomy surreys, drawn by lighter breeds of horses. Some of the early carriage makers in Richmond included Lippincott, Schneider, Cramer, Crocker and Stratton. Several livery stables rented out rigs.

Horses provided city transport in Richmond. They pulled the delivery wagons, the doctor's buggy, the ice wagon and the passengers. A favorite memory of some is the faithful milk wagon horse that knew his route so well that the delivery man could carry his supply basket to two or three houses before going back to the wagon for a refill. The horse knew when to go and where to stop.

While the Richmond area enjoyed an abundant supply of streams to power the mills, the streams were too shallow for boat traffic. The success of the Erie Canal across upper New York state, completed in 1825, was an incentive to attempt similar projects in Ohio and Indiana. A canal could provide a means to send farm produce east and bring passengers and manufactured goods to the western settlements at lower cost than overland travel.

The Whitewater Valley Canal was proposed from Hagerstown south through Cambridge City and Brookville to the Ohio River and the major port of Cincinnati. Digging, shoring up sides and lock-making were completed to Hagerstown by 1847. In order to be included in this project it was necessary to form the Richmond and Brookville Canal Company in 1838. The directors planned to dig a canal bed nearly parallel to the East fork of the Whitewater River about 34 miles to the junction of the large West fork at Brookville.

Unfortunately this plan washed out with the floodwaters of January 1847. The walls and locks of the Whitewater Valley Canal were ruined and the $45,000 invested in the shorter canal was lost.

The National Road

After bumping over the corduroy roads in a wagon or carriage, the traveler on the National Road was glad to see the welcoming sign of the Neal Tavern when he crossed the state line from Ohio. Being several miles east of the city center, the tavern was also a post office for the eastern part of Wayne Township. The five-bay Federal-style brick with its "ell" on the south side could accommodate those who wanted a quick meal, taken perhaps at the long table in the main room while the weary horses were being changed for fresh ones.

The traveler who was tired of the jouncing ride could even rent a room or, if the tavern were crowded, share a room with three or four others. The driver would often find a place to nap on the hay in the barn.

Christian Buhl

Christian Buhl's tavern (later in its history to become Richmond Auto Parts), located at the west edge of Richmond, could refresh the traveler from the west who had just crossed the Whitewater River, or prepare the traveler about to go west. It was later the site of the Minck Brewery when Buhl and his wife, Sarah, retired to their farm southwest of the city. He had come from Germany in 1830 and married Sarah Stripe in 1839.

The building has been demolished in recent years.

Joseph C. Ratliff (1827-1909) was the son of Cornelius Ratliff, Jr., an early Quaker settler who came from North Carolina. Their ancestor, Joseph Ratliff, came from England with William Penn.

Joseph studied first at the Richmond Academy with the goal of teaching. After a year or so of the academic life, he decided to study dentistry, then medicine. In 1854 he joined Milo Shinn and Timothy Thistlethwaite in a papermaking mill venture on the West fork of the Whitewater. He became a trustee of Purdue University and served as president, superintendent and treasurer of the Wayne County Turnpike Company, chartered in the winter of 1849-50. This lasted until control of the roads was taken over by the county and its townships. Ratliff was also one of the founders of the Wayne County Horticultural Society.

"The East-West Main Street of the United States"

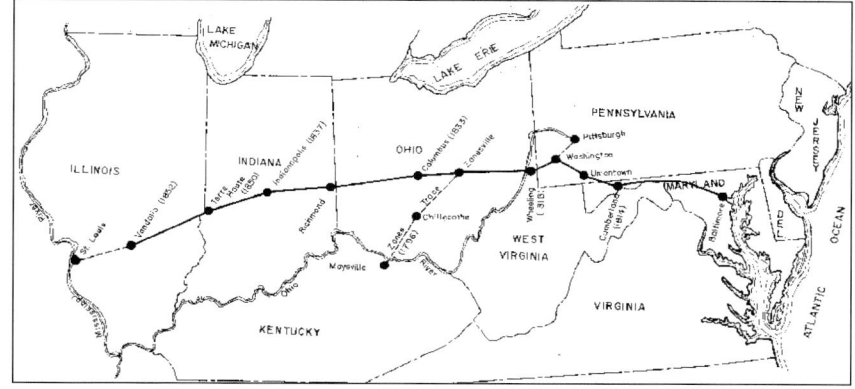

This map shows the development of the National Road which was used by those forging their way westward.

The Whitewater River gorge was a formidable barrier to vehicles going west from Richmond. Oriented north and south, it required early travelers to find a shallow fording place, usually near the base of South Mill, later D Street. Using limestone from Abington, south of Richmond, stonemasons built strong abutments for a two-lane covered bridge in 1834. Graceful arches for the two lanes plus walkways on each side marked the two ends. The bridge was in service until 1893.

By 1893 a person on the west side of the river could look over Conrad Winkler's dyeing and cleaning establishment to the tower of the firehouse and City building at left and the Richardsonian Romanesque Wayne County courthouse, at right.

The Railroad

By 1845 Richmond and Wayne County settlers had heard of the success of railroads which were not dependent on vagaries of rainfall (i.e. Whitewater Valley Canal fiasco) but used steam for power. Wood to fuel the engines was readily available and water to produce the steam could be stored in tanks at regular intervals or even bucketed out of ditches along the rails. The first local railroad, the Richmond and Miami, was incorporated that same year, 1846. and a branch line was added to connect with the Dayton and Western Railroad at the state line. Regular train service started in Richmond on September 19, 1853.

Oldtimers recall relatives who told them about the crowd that lined the west side of the Whitewater Gorge to watch the first locomotive cross the railroad bridge. There was a tense moment when the engineer started across, then a great cheer when the bridge held its load. The engineer backed up to attach the tender carrying the fuel and water, then crossed the chasm to the roar of the crowd.

Names of railroads changed rapidly as small local lines formed, then were bought up by larger lines. Gradually, Richmond had rails connecting to Terre Haute, Chicago, Cincinnati, and all points east and west, north and south. The Chicago, St. Louis & Pittsburgh became known locally as the Pan-Handle railroad, and Richmond even boasted a Pan-Handle grocery.

The locomotive pictured above circa 1865 is reported to be the first steam type in Richmond. The Terre Haute & Richmond Railroad Company was chartered on January 26, 1847, to build rails from Terre Haute through Indianapolis to Richmond. On January 20, 1851, by act of the State legislature, the lines were ended at Indianapolis. A new company, the Indiana Central Railway, was formed to build from the state capitol to Richmond. Samuel Hanna was president from March to July of 1851 and was followed by his son-in-law, John S. Newman of Centerville, a nephew of David Hoover, the surveyor and one of Richmond's founders. The line became the Chicago, St. Louis & Pittsburgh.

Notice above: As early as 1846 Richmond citizens had recovered from "canal fever" and were being urged to consider construction of "our railroad." The Warner building on North 5th Sreet was a gift of Dr. Ithamar Warner, early physician.

Workmen in 1900 construct the Cincinnati, Richmond & Muncie Railroad. Overseeing the work is T. W. Allen, second from left. This was the last steam line built in Wayne County and became part of the Chesapeake & Ohio system. With several railroads serving the city, Trade increased tremendously.

The Chesapeake & Ohio Railroad, the Chessie, built its station on North 3rd Street and served such companies as Starr Piano, Richmond Baking Company and Gaar, Scott &Co. The Nixon paper mill is visible in the valley at left.

Where the C&O tracks (right) crossed the East Fork of the Whitewater River it was close to the Nixon Paper Mill. That mill, for the most part, made paper bags.

A metal bridge over the Whitewater River (below) replaced the wooden covered bridge about 1893, but it was considered too weak to carry trolley and Interurban cars. A temporary bridge was built directly south of the main structure for the metal tracks.

A handsome French Second Empire style was featured in the design of Union Station on North E Street. The site for the station was donated in 1850 by Charles W. Starr.

A large train shed protected the railroad cars and passengers at the station. Adjacent businesses included the Adam H. Bartel Wholesale Company, the Arlington Hotel and Phares Drugstore on North E Street.

A new railway station was constructed in 1894 from a design by Fred Burnham of the Daniel Burnham Company of Chicago. It was built of brick over a sturdy metal framework and has massive columns facing North E Street. Decorative detail is done in terra cotta.

A favorite pastime for many Richmond residents was going down to the depot to watch the trains pull in. The whistle of the steam locomotive such as the Strasburg was a sound remembered with nostalgia by Richmond train buffs for years to come.

A bridge for auto traffic over North E Street and the railroad tracks was needed, especially for ambulances to reach Reid Memorial Hospital north of the tracks. The overpass was sited at North 9th Street about 25 years ago. In addition to the bridge itself, a gentle approach was constructed from the south.

Like the taverns of the National Road, the railroad station provided food for travelers. While railroad aficionados were waiting for an engine to admire they, too, could enjoy a cup of coffee and a piece of pie.

At the Pennsy Station the restaurant was situated at the west end of the building. One could even discuss genealogy and local history with genial Frank Dolloff, a descendant of Jeremiah Cox, one of Richmond's founders.

A major support for the railroad bridge across the Whitewater River consists of river rock from the Ordovician period. This metal bridge represents the second railroad bridge over the river.

Horses were essential to the everyday movement of the city. Livery stables at convenient locations were the equivalent of today's cab companies and parking garages. Thomas Rose's stable was at 1119-1121 East Main Street. After trying dentistry and running a notions store Rose returned to his first love—horses. He operated a sales and boarding stable from 1886 to 1895. Rose was also a veteran of the Civil War conflict.

The famous pacer, Single G, a great-grandson of George Wilkes of the Hambletonian line, was raised on a farm west of Richmond and provided entertainment for harness racing fans who came many miles to see his races. He was foaled April 4, 1910, retired from racing at the age of 16, and died at 25 years. Curt Gosnell is driving here, in 1916. Most county fairgrounds had half-mile driving tracks.

Richmond's Santa Clauses arrive in various ways, with preference given to a sled even when there is no snow. McConaha's Garage at South 4th and Main streets provided the background for a sled on wheels.

A four-horse hitch was needed to pull the large tallyho used by groups of revelers. Here the vehicle crosses the trolley tracks at 8th and Main streets near the Union National Bank. The earliest streetcars were also horse-drawn.

Instead of renting delivery wagons, many stores maintained their own vehicles and teams. One such venture was the Romey Furniture Store established by William H. Romey in 1905 at 927 Main Street. Born in Bluffton, Romey's parents came to America from Switzerland.

The Richmond Baking Company was started at 13 South 5th street by David J. Hoerner (1830-1895). A native of Waldenburg, Germany, Hoerner emigrated to Dayton and apprenticed in the Bosler & Bowman Bakery. Before the turn of the century, a baker's wagon brought fresh breads, pies and cakes to the housewife's door.

The two-horse sprinkler was a welcome sight as it helped to lay the dust on Richmond's unpaved streets.

The Railsback family's arrival in the Richmond area dates to 1807 when David and Sarah Stevens Railsback came to Abington from North Carolina. Their son, Enoch, born in North Carolina, later owned a farm near the site of Salisbury, first seat of Wayne County. Note that the horses are protected from biting flies by fringed netting as they haul sacks of wheat.

The horse-drawn milk wagon with its alert horses provided an important delivery service when city dwellers no longer kept their own dairy cows. The early boulder gutter is visible at the edge of the unpaved street. This is North B Street facing North 15th Street.

The Wayne Agricultural Company was started by Caleb W. Witt of Dublin in 1837, and made sickles and scythes. In 1875 L. L. Lawrence and David Sutton moved the firm to Richmond and added wagons, buggies and carriages to their inventory. The school hack proved to be a popular model.

Streetcars

In the city the trolley line became a convenient way of connecting most neighborhoods with the center of commerce. Horses drew the cars until overhead electric wires were installed. The latter sometimes sparked and sputtered, frightening the populace. Open cars were put on the track in summer and closed ones for cold weather.

At the end of each route, the backs of the seats could be moved by the conductor or motorman so that no one had to ride backwards. Lines reached to Glen Miller Park, a popular destination on the east side, and to Earlham College on the west.

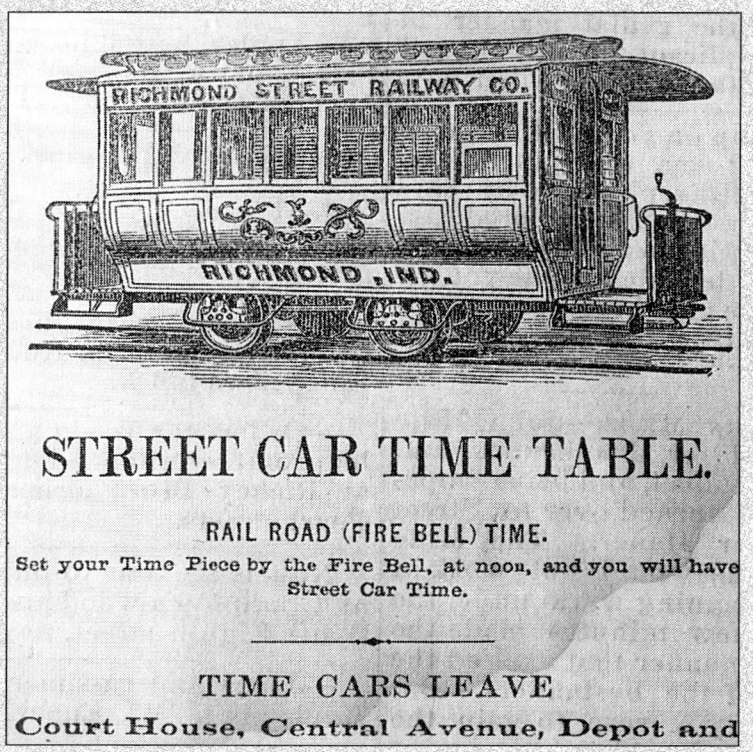

Streetcars were economical for those who didn't own a carriage and a great convenience for shoppers. At first they were drawn by teams of horses, and later were powered by electricity via the "trolley" mechanism.

The horsecar ticket indicates the half hour schedule on the streetcar line between the college and the shopping center of the city.

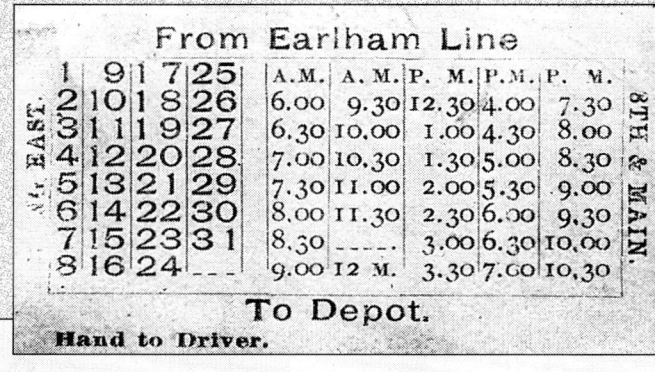

The tall pole on top of the car shows that the Main St. & Earlham car was powered by the overhead electrified wire. Earlham Hall is at the south end of the entrance drive and Lindley Hall is at right.

Summer streetcars with their open sides provided natural breezes. There were roll-down curtains for protection from showers or too much sun.

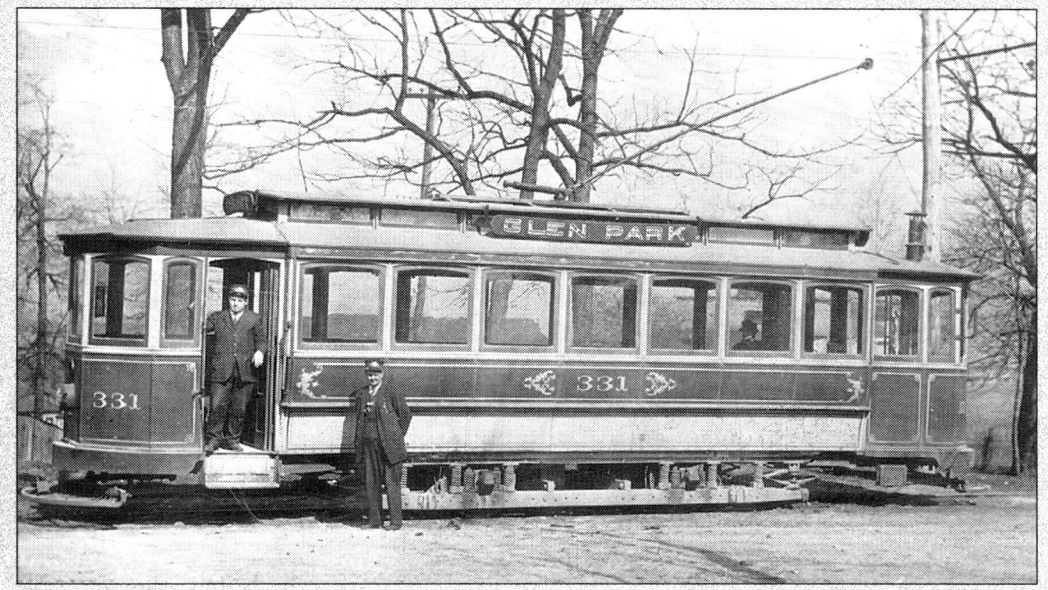

In cooler weather patrons riding this circa 1900 streetcar enjoyed glass windows protecting them from the elements. Jesse Jarrett in the car was motorman, and Jesse Stevens, conductor.

At the 8th and Main streets intersection, one could find the electric trolley, horse-drawn buggies and wagons about 1896 when looking east. The towered Kelly-Hutchinson Building is at right.

Another convenient mode of transportation was the Interurban line. A traveler could cross Indiana from Richmond to Terre Haute or go east to Dayton, Ohio. The Interurban tracks, for the most part, paralleled the National Road. The trains reached the towns along the route on a regular schedule.

The Interurban

The use of electricity made possible the Interurbans which resembled large trolley cars. A traveler could go from Dayton to Terre Haute with cars leaving on half-hour schedules. One could even leave the car at Lewisville or Knightstown, perhaps, have a cup of coffee or an ice cream cone, then board the next car to Richmond or Indianapolis. The independence that drivers gained through use of the personal automobile, however, sounded the death knell for the Interurbans. The last car ran in Richmond on a Saturday night, April 23, 1938.

The junction of 8th and Main streets has long been a busy intersection. It was a crossing or turning point for streetcars, and was the site of the Second National Bank, at left, and Dickinson Trust Company, at right.

Buses

The Trailways Bus Company used the Rex Hotel as its depot. It was located at 5th and Main streets. Joe Cloud, hotel manager for many years, later became head of Indiana's Department of Natural Resources.

In March of 1937 there were two major changes in the city's transportation system. The legal receiver of the former streetcar company asked to replace the streetcars with buses; the Pennsylvania Greyhound Line, Inc., made plans to convert the former terminal of the traction company on South 8th Street to a bus depot.

The Automobile

With many machinists and machine shops in the city, it is only natural that the automobile was a topic of great interest. Mr. and Mrs. Al Speckenhier appear happy in what was recognized as "the first car in Richmond."

The Westcott Motor Car Company manufactured an auto labeled Westcott from 1909 to 1916. Here the large 1912 touring car is being driven by Ruth Tyler Hough.

The Rodefeld Company started as a blacksmith shop that branched out into auto parts. They made trucks and also the Rodefeld touring car from 1905 to 1917.

The lure of the open (though often muddy and rutted) road was not to be denied. Families often traveled in tandem as are the Micajah Henley family in the front car with the Clem Gaar family bringing up the rear. That arrangement ensured there was always more help with a flat tire.

Richmond, with its blacksmiths, carriage makers and tool shops was not left behind in the production of personal vehicles. A total of 14 automobiles has been listed as made in Richmond. They include:

Richmond, 1901-16, Wayne Works Corp.
Sedgwick, 1901, I. H. Sedgwick Co.
Richmond Steam, 1902-03, Richmond Auto & Cycle Co.
Wayne, 1904, Wayne Works Corp.
Rodefeld, 1905-17, Rodefeld Co. (trucks and a touring car)
Westcott, 1909-16, Westcott Motor Car Co.
Davis, 1909-28. G. W. Davis Corp.
Pilot, 1909-24, Pilot Motor Car Co.
E.I.M., 1915-16, Eastern Motor Car Corp.
Laurel, 1916-17, Laurel Motor Car Co.
Utility, 1918, Utility Car Co.
Lorrain, 1920-23, Lorrain Motor Car Co.
New York Six, 1928-29, Automobile Corp. of America.
Crosley, 1939-41, Crosley Motors Inc.

On display at the Wayne County Historical Museum are five of the locally made cars, the Richmond, Westcott, Davis, Pilot and Crosley.

The more exotic form of transport, the airplane, was also made in Richmond.

Mayor William W. Zimmerman presents to the camera his large touring car at the entrance to Glen Miller park.

The Wayne Agricultural Company in 1888 became the Wayne Works with William G. Scott as president. In addition to planters, seeders and discs, it manufactured many types of wagons and eventually specialized in school buses. The company exhibited its 4-cylinder automobile, the *Richmond*, at the 1905 Chicago Auto Fair.

Trucks at Work

Motorized delivery wagons were becoming popular by the time this Starr Piano wagon was used.

Forrest Monger demonstrated his expertise in loading furniture onto a stake truck with heavy chests and dressers below, then mattresses, bed frames and chairs above.

By having a large tarpaulin with the company name, Monger neatly covered the load of furniture and also created an advertising sign.

Pictured is another Monger truck of the same time period, (when telephone numbers had four digits). The vehicle is parked front of the International Harvester Company which came to Richmond in 1903.

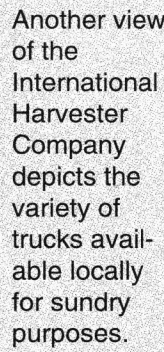

Another view of the International Harvester Company depicts the variety of trucks available locally for sundry purposes.

Chapter 3

A large number of early settlers came to the Wayne County area of eastern Indiana to buy and farm the land. The coming of the farmer was precursor to the beginning of the agricultural machine industry. At first a farmer relied on his woodworking skills to make hay forks and oxen yokes, but soon there was a demand for metal sickles, scythe blades, metal plows and harrows.

Fortunately there were businessmen who possessed both imagination and skill to start companies. Isaac Jones was one of these entrepreneurs. He came from a Welsh family, and started a stove foundry in 1836. He also was successful in raising silkworms on a small scale. Early newspapers carried ads encouraging people to grow Morus multicaulus, the mulberry tree whose leaves were eaten by the silkworm larvae. (This is considered to be a variety of white mulberry, Morus alba and originated in Asia.)

Jones named his metal business the Spring Foundry because of the natural spring on the east bank of the Whitewater River that provided power for the business. By 1839 Jones was ready to sell the foundry to Jesse M. and John H. Hutton, brothers who came from Maryland. In 1841 this foundry built a chaff-piler, the first thresher made in Indiana.

Employees of the Spring Foundry included Jonas Gaar, his two sons, Abram and John Milton Gaar, and a son-in-law, William Scott. When they asked for

Three steam engines made by Gaar, Scott & Company were moved by teams of horses or mules.

Business in Richmond

a raise in salary, they were given shares in the foundry instead. The firm name was changed to A. Gaar & Co. in 1849, while the Huttons changed their focus to casket making. The foundry became known as Gaar, Scott & Company and gradually gained a world-wide clientele.

Another machine company was begun in 1842 by Francis Robinson, also a native of Maryland. Like many machinists, he learned carpentry before shifting to metalwork; the reason being that wooden molds were usually made before metal was cast at a foundry. Henry E. Robinson succeeded his father as president and took in his brother-in-law, S. E. Swayne. The firm is reported to be the oldest gray iron casting company under the same name in the United States.

Although the early settlers made their own furniture or brought a few pieces with them from homes farther east or south, there soon was a need for chairs, tables, desks and church pews. Millers, tanners, wagon and carriage makers and even shoe peg-makers were in demand.

Human resources were also in demand. Businesses large and small required skilled workers to run them. The community also needed professionals such as lawyers and doctors. Hotels were raised to accommodate visitors and traveling salesmen. Bankers were called on to handle the finances of the burgeoning town.

The city was thriving and growing.

Gaar, Scott & Company

Gaar, Scott & Company has been one of Richmond's most well-known firms. It has won gold medals at agricultural shows and fairs, and shipped its products all over the world. In 1911 it became part of the Rumley Manufacturing Company of LaPorte, Indiana. Very little was produced after that merger and the Richmond Commercial Club bought the property in March, 1916. The buildings in Richmond were gradually taken over by other local firms.

Jonas Gaar (1793-1875), his sons, Abram (1819-1894) and John M. (1823-1900), and Jonas' son-in-law, William G. Scott (1824-1897), each received a one-fifth share of the Spring Foundry from the Hutton brothers in lieu of a raise in salary.

Isaac Jones from Ohio was a tailor who began the Spring Foundry and also owned a silk factory. When the silk business failed Isaac bought the machinery in 1845 and moved it to Newport, Kentucky.

The Gaar, Scott & Company employed many skilled machinists in their foundry located north of the railroad tracks. Son often followed father in the employ of the company.

A. Gaar & Company exhibited its portable threshing machine at the Indiana State Fair in the summer of 1868. The chimney stack could be folded down to fit through a barn door.

The early office of Gaar, Scott & Company was built in 1865. The flaring cornice and low pitched roof reflect an Italianate architectural influence.

The Romanesque Revival style headquarters, designed by John Hasecoster for Gaar, Scott & Company, was later home to the Richmond Baking Company and is currently in use by the firm in 1994.

A typical threshing scene shows the steam engine at left in the photo, the belt for power take-off leading to the wagon loaded with wheat, to the right. The dusty chaff emerges as the waste and grain are separated near the horse-drawn wagon at right.

Threshing

Over 6,000 threshing machines were being used by Indiana farmers in 1919. The threshing process, separating the heads of wheat, oats or barley from the stalks, was all-important to the harvest season. Threshermen would not let their machines be idle but would go from farm to farm for work. W. H. Newsom, president of the Indiana Brotherhood of Threshermen, came to Richmond in April, 1919, to encourage the threshers to organize. The membership at that time numbered 3,200. The meeting was held at the Commercial Club.

Newsom praised the local organization as one of the best in the state. Officers elected were: William Doynes, Centerville, president; John Clevenger, Centerville, vice-president; and Alva E. Alexander, Whitewater, secretary-treasurer.

Everyone on a farm pitched in at threshing time. The work often had to be completed between rain showers. The men and boys did the heavy work while women and girls prepared meals for the threshing ring, so-called because the group moved from farm to farm. One youngster was in charge of carrying a jug of water, lemonade or "hay-makers switchel" to the workers. Switchel was a refreshing drink which was made with a vinegar base.

Solomon Beard and William Sinex advertised its Indiana Steam Agricultural Works in the Richmond City Directory of 1857. At the Indiana State Fair of 1855 the company won silver cups and $25 for farm implements such as its corn-sheller, harrow, cultivator, straw cutter, and a plow designed for Indiana soils. Silver cups and $10 were awarded for the firm's prairie plow, subsoil plow and horse rake.

In 1903 International Harvester came to Richmond seeking space for a factory. Not finding what they wanted, they built a substantial brick factory on the north side of North E Street, and employed a large work force.

Swayne, Robinson & Co.

Distinguished as the oldest, family-owned foundry in the United States and Richmond's oldest industry, Swayne, Robinson & Co. was founded in 1842 by Francis W. Robinson (1810-1897). The oldest of seven children, Robinson probably learned carpentry from his father. After spending a few years in Ohio, he came to Richmond and opened his foundry on the north side of Main Street between Second and Third streets.

The second president was Henry E. Robinson, Francis' Son (1839-1909). The third to take over the helm was Samuel E. (Ed) Swayne, (Francis W.'s son-in-law) who became a partner when the firm was incorporated in 1889.

About 1900 the agricultural equipment manufacturing business underwent a shaking-out period similar to the automobile industry with the resulting survivors being John Deere, International Harvester, etc. Unable to compete, the founder's grandson, H. R. Robinson developed the iron casting portion of the business.

In 1994 the firm remains in the original location and is still in the Robinson family with 7th generation, Charles Robinson, Jr., serving as president.

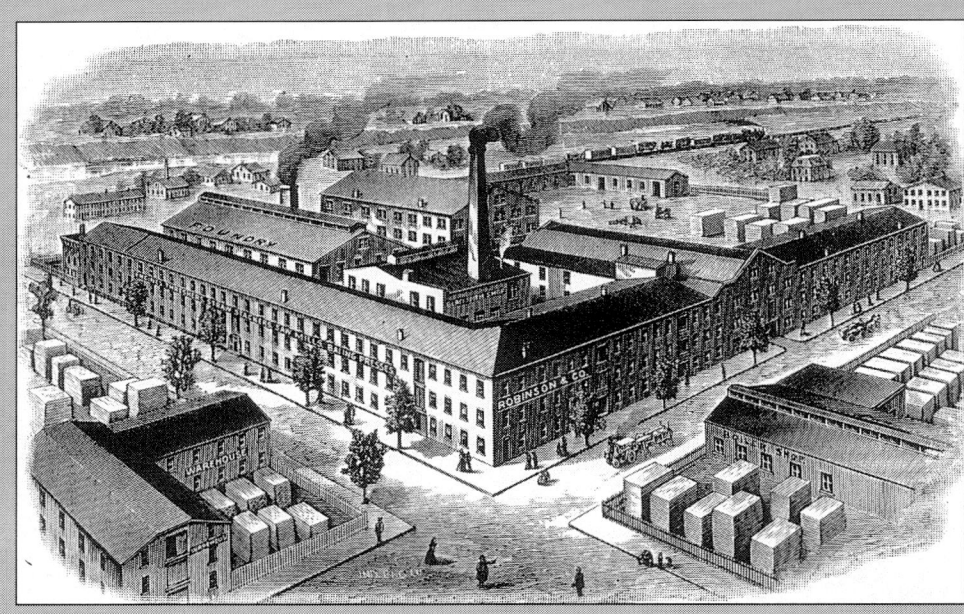

View in 1900 of the Swayne, Robinson Company from a company flyer.

A corner of the Swayne, Robinson Company factory at Third and Main streets about 1910.

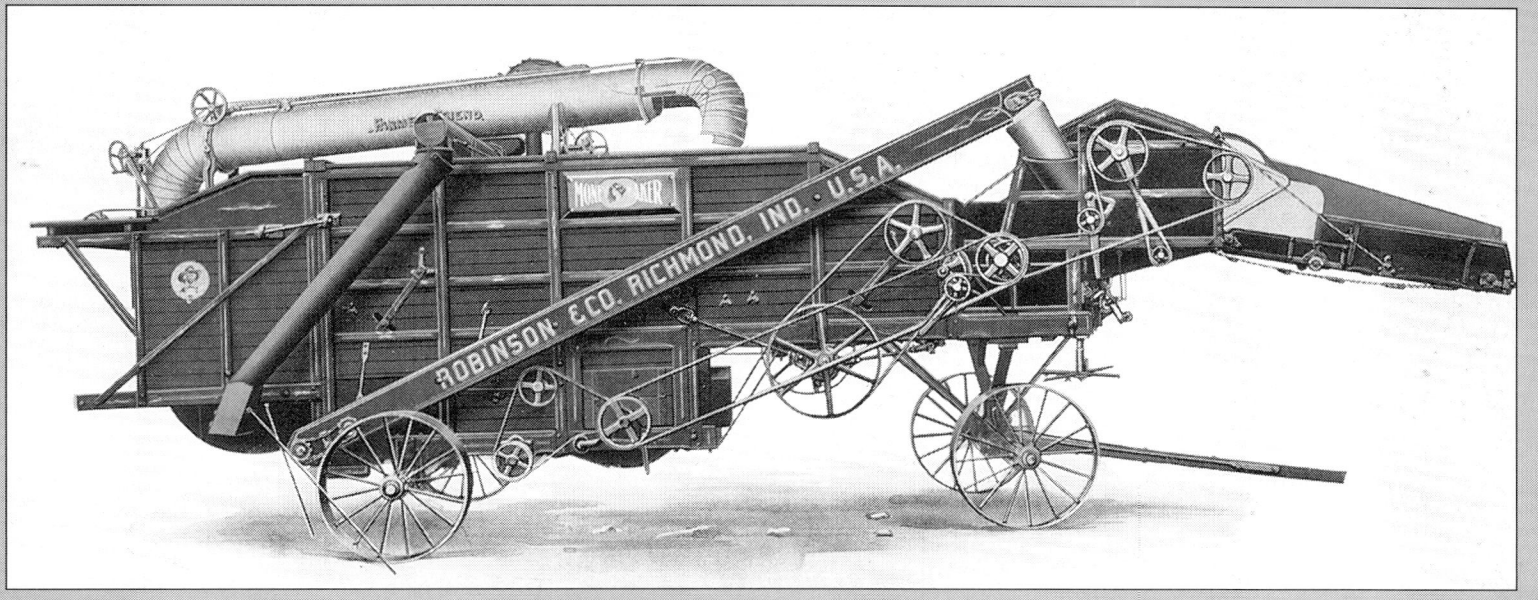

Accurate and attractive drawings of products were illustrated in the Swayne, Robinson & Company advertising booklet.

The self-feeding baler was designed to speed baling of hay and straw by reducing the number of men needed for the task.

The Casket Business

Richmond and neighboring communities had access to a plentiful supply of hardwood which became converted to log houses and furniture with the scrap wood burned for fuel. Carpenters, joiners and cabinet makers had the tools and expertise to make the body's final container, the coffin. One of the softwoods, pine, might have been used, but poplar, beech and other woods were abundant. Black walnut, maple and cherry were probably reserved for architectural interiors. Metalworkers were available to make casket hardware when coffins became more elaborate and an industry developed that exported coffins to other cities. Preparing the linings for coffins was considered a suitable job for women and seamstresses were employed at most casket factories.

Ezra and James Smith made window sashes, shutters and doors in addition to coffins in 1864 at the northeast corner of 9th and South A streets.

The Ezra Smith Company grew into the four-story brick factory of the Richmond Coffin and Casket Works at 9th and South A streets. This location is the current site of the Leland Hotel.

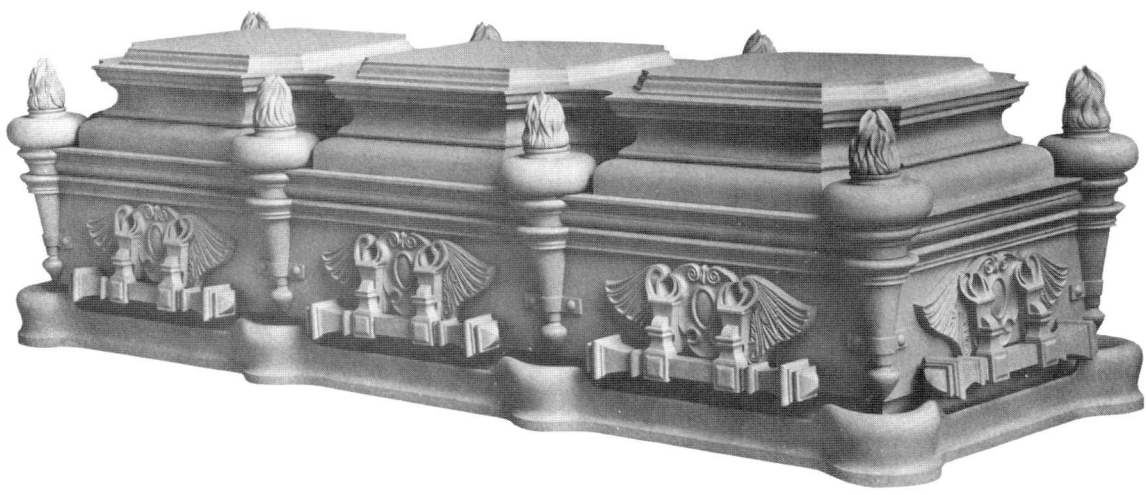

Pictured is a sample of an ornate, sculptured casket, designed by Jesse M. Hutton Company. Evidently affordable only to the wealthy, the common man had the option of selecting a simpler and less expensive style.

Jesse M. Hutton and his brother, John, started their casket company after selling their foundry to the Gaar family. The firm is located at 12th and North E streets. It is reported to be the oldest hardwood casket company operating under the same name in the country. In 1872 it was manufacturing over 11,000 coffins a year.

A group of J. M. Hutton & Company workers shows a range of ages, including young boys. Child labor laws were enacted several times in the early twentieth century, but then repealed until the Fair Labor Standards Act was passed in 1938.

49

Starr Piano

In 1872 George Trayser needed financial help with his struggling business of building pianos. Richard Jackson and James M. Starr of Richmond were willing to invest in Trayser's project and the piano company moved from Ohio to Richmond. This firm became the Chase Piano Company in 1878, James Starr & Company in 1881, and finally Starr Piano Company, Inc. in 1893.

Although the pay was often not as high as in some other factories, men seemed to feel that working at the Starr had advantages. The work was steady and if a man wanted time off in squirrel season no one would object. Moreover, as a craftsman, a man could take pride in the creation of a beautiful instrument.

The Whitewater Valley has been associated with music for many years, first with the Valley Gem Piano Company, then the Trayser Company. The two merged as Chase Piano until Benjamin Starr, Henry Gennett and John Lumsden formed the Starr Piano Company in 1893.

Workers at Starr Piano composed a variety of specialists including those who could manipulate a piano's hammers and strings; those who made the pedals work and the woodworkers who sanded, stained and polished the wooden cases to a high shine.

A large staff of office workers and salesmen, shown in 1912, handled the marketing and recordkeeping for the Starr Piano Company. For many families, a piano in the living room was a visible indication of music appreciation.

Experienced wood-carvers were hired, usually from Europe, to make the master patterns for the Starr piano cases.

Some organs were displayed along with Starr pianos at the spacious showroom at the southwest corner of 10th and Main streets.

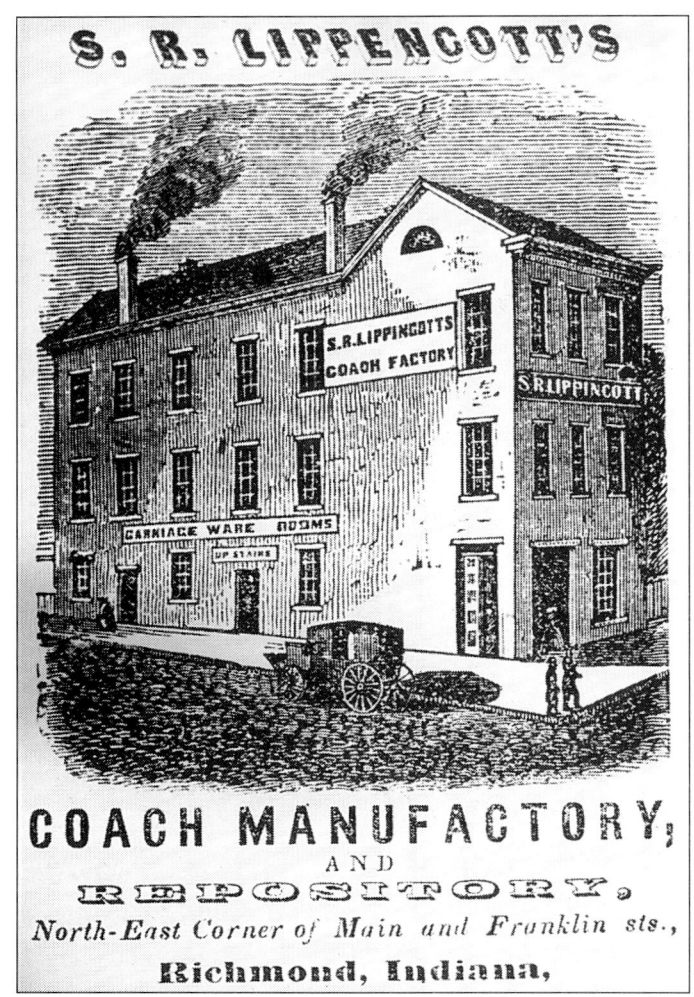

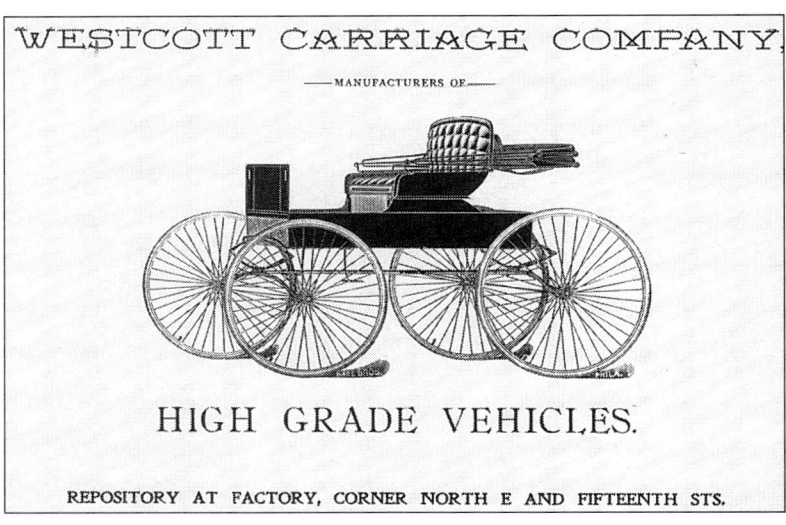

This product of the Westcott Carriage Company was known as a spring wagon.

Samuel Lippincott apprenticed for seven years in Philadelphia with a first-rate carriage maker, according to his advertisement in the *Richmond Palladium* in 1848. In later years he owned an undertaking establishment, started about 1881, and sold in 1888 to G. F. Baker.

After the dissolution of the Wayne Agricultural Company in 1888, the Wayne Works bought two of the older firm's buildings. First officers of the new company were William G. Scott, Howard Campbell, W. W. Schultz and E. B. Clements. In addition to farm implements, they manufactured a variety of wagons, depot hacks and platform drays. Its Richmond motor car had an electric starter instead of the old hand crank and a clutch of its own design. The car was displayed at the Chicago auto show of 1905.

F & N Lawnmowers

The F & N Lawn Mower Company was named for William Farmer and Finley Newlin. Its mower used a ratchet invented and patented by Farmer. The factory was north of the railroad tracks near North E Street. Newlin started the business in 1887, and it was incorporated in 1895 with John M. Gaar as president, Howard Campbell, vice-president, Daniel G. Reid, treasurer, and John M. Lontz, secretary. They purchased three former Gaar, Scott & Company buildings as part of the factory.

The Dille & McGuire Manufacturing Company demonstrated their lawn movers at Chicago's Columbian Exposition of 1893 with a large crew of men. Their first lawn movers were produced in 1874.

F & N Lawn Mower Company was located north of the Pennsylvania Railroad tracks at 540 North 8th Street.

Company officials admire their product.

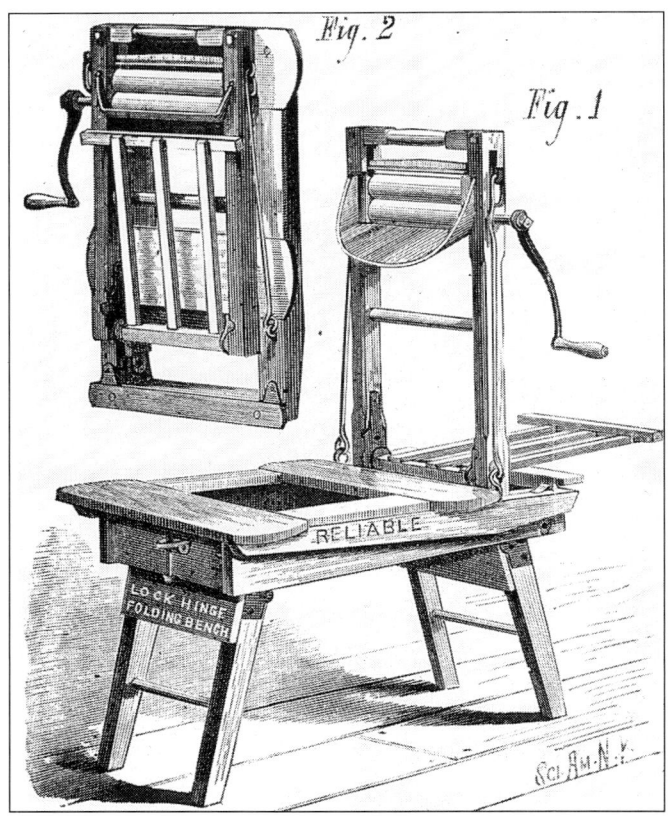

James Kaighn Dugdale (1815-1892) held a patent on a laundry wringer, illustrated in an issue of *Scientific American* magazine in 1882. He was born in Haddonfield, New Jersey and came to Richmond in 1834, to be followed in 1837 by his parents and brothers, Thomas and Samuel.

The Adam H. Bartel Company building (below) is located at 911-921 North E Street. The firm was founded in 1877 by Adam Bartel who was soon joined in business by John M. Coate (1858-1940) as vice-president. Coate came to Richmond as a very young man from Fountain City. Descendants of both men remain in Richmond and are involved in the business.

The O. B. Rowlett Desk Company manufactured both flat and roll-top desks, but apparently did not stay in business longer than 15 years. In 1896 Oliver B. Rowlett was president of the firm with Harry C. Keelor as vice-president and superintendent and M. L. Strattan served as secretary-treasurer. Business losses caused reorganization in 1897 with Daniel G. Reid as president, James A. Coffin, vice-president, John H. Cutter, secretary, and O. B. Rowlett as general superintendent. In 1906 George H. Knollenberg bought controlling interest, and in 1910 sold the building at North 10th and J streets to the Watt & Keelor Casket Company.

Adam H. Bartel (1850-1942), founder of the wholesale drygoods company named for him, was born at Astrup, Kingdom of Hanover (Germany). He came to Richmond in 1854. His marriage in 1875 to Matilda Knollenberg united two important merchandising families of the city.

Atlas Underwear was built at North 10th and D streets in 1919. A central atrium and large windows provided light to all parts of the factory, and the company's ads were worded to encourage women to apply for work. During World War II Atlas specialized in underwear for the U. S. Army and later supplied some of the special suits worn by U. S. astronauts.

Richmond Fireproof Door was located on North West F Street. Recently the building has served as headquarters for Hoffco Inc., makers of weed cutters and other garden tools.

Champion Roller Mill was constructed in 1877 by William Kendall and I. M. Barnes as an oil mill. It was powered by steam and converted to a flouring mill in circa 1883. Using a patented roller process its capacity was 200 barrels of flour in 24 hours.

At the left, the tall Knollenberg Building at 809 Main Street had been built in 1877, and the *Item* newspaper was in the adjoining building to the west. The typical cigar store Indian guards S. M. Buckley's establishment. The corner was later occupied by the massive Kelly-Hutchinson Building, and, in 1935, by a modern Kresge store. In 1977 Birck's Hardware moved into the former Kresge space.

Knollenberg's

Knollenberg's is one of those great hometown stores where an industrious family was successful in providing clothing and household goods to several generations of local families. George Knollenberg was born in Richmond of parents who had come from Astrup in the Kingdom of Hanover, (later to unite as Germany). After three short years of selling notions and fancy goods on the south side of Main Street between 5th and 6th streets. he opened his own business a few blocks east. He expanded, erected two buildings on Main Street and an annex on South 8th. He was always considerate of his family and employed many relatives.

George H. Knollenberg (1847-1918) began his commercial career at the age of 14 years by working in the Emswiler & Crocker drygoods store. After three years as a clerk, he was able to establish his own store in a one-story building at 809 Main Street.

The employers and the employed at Knollenberg's includes George H. Knollenberg and other company officers in the front row. In the background is the impressive 1877 building.

The 1877 building at the right in the photo carries the architectural style developed by Charles Eastlake. The adjacent 1888 building is characterized by the Queen Anne style. Both structures were designed by John A. Hasecoster (1844-1925), born in Osnabrueck, Hanover.

When making a purchase in Knollenberg's, money was given to the clerk who placed it—with the bill of sale—in a small container. This was then sent by the wire system to the cashier on an upper floor or mezzanine, where any change was made and returned to the clerk below.

Expansion of business led to the erection of Knollenberg's annex in 1896 and also eliminated the saloon that had been on South 8th Street.

Birck's Hardware

The story of Birck's Ace Hardware turns back to 1794 with the birth of Daniel P. Wiggans in Jericho, New York, on the western part of Long Island. He mastered the tanning business there and became acquainted with Elias Hicks, Quaker farmer and abolitionist.

Daniel (1794-1875), his wife, Phoebe, and five children came to Richmond in 1823, carrying a letter of recommendation from Hicks. Wiggans readily found work at the tannery of Robert Morrisson and in 1826, was welcomed as a partner.

By 1846 Wiggans, with several of his sons, was able to purchase the John Smith tannery from the pioneer settler. Daniel retired in 1851 leaving the tannery and leather business to his son, Stephen, who separated the two operations. The store with leather items at 509 Main Street was sold in 1906 to Philip Birck, harness dealer from Madison, Indiana.

About this time Philip Birck bought his well-known trademark, a model horse named Jocko, 15 hands high and made of water-resistant pulp with metal ears. Looking life-size, Jocko could wear the latest items of tack from the saddler and harness maker. He was often part of the Birck's float in parades.

In 1914 Philip Birck (1861-1836) bought the harness shop of Charles Keys at 616 Main Street. Philip and his son, Alfred (1885-1871), then ran both stores before combining them as Philip Birck & Son at 507-509 Main Street. Another move, in 1921, found them at 609-611 Main Street and in 1962 Alfred expanded the stock by purchasing the contents of Hornaday Hardware.

The shop at 609-611 Main Street, heavily damaged by the explosion and fire of April 6, 1968, was moved once again to 718 Main Street. In 1977 Charles Maurer, senior, president of Philip Birck & Son, Inc., moved to larger quarters at 801 Promenade where the Kelly-Hutchinson building had once stood.

Jocko the horse joins the staff of the Birck harness store in front of the shop at 509 Main Street, once Wiggans harness shop. Left to right are Bill McNally and Charles Seifert, harness makers; and Philip Birck and his son, Alfred.

Philip Birck, at left, is in his store at 609-611 Main Street. Bill McNally, the harness maker, stands at far right.

Wayne Dairy

Wayne Dairy Products Company was organized in May, 1921, by 150 dairymen forming a co-operative venture. John M. Haas served as first president. In 1923, at the second annual meeting, Joseph Hill, then president, reminded those present that a major aim was to merchandise milk products instead of dumping them on the market. By combining their efforts they could obtain better return on their labor.

Standardization of the fat content, cleanliness of the farms and careful temperature control were of primary importance. The processing plant was at South 6th and A streets, and by 1930 the directors decided to double its size. Butter was sold as "Quality" brand and other products were whipping cream, cottage cheese, condensed milk and buttermilk. James L. Dolan acted as manager for 25 years.

During this era many in mid-America had enlarged thyroid glands, a condition known as goiter, because of lack of iodine in their diet. Rose Hill Milk was developed for children and invalids by Joe Hill at his Rose Hill Farm on Pleasant View Road. Seaweed, high in iodine, was added to the cows' feed to raise the iodine content of the milk. This milk was processed separately and sold under a special label. Today extra iodine is often included in table salt.

A Wayne Dairy pamphlet of 1930 reminded customers that early morning delivery, starting at 2 a.m., should not disturb sleepers because rubber tires were replacing steel ones on the wagons and the horseshoes were also of rubber. Over the years, several other dairies were purchased and ice cream production was added.

In 1978 the plant moved to 1590 North West 11th Street. In the 1979 Richmond Rose Festival Wayne Dairy contributed 300 gallons of vanilla ice cream to top pieces of the 10-foot diameter peach pie baked in a huge oven.

The Wayne Dairy soda fountain at South 6th and A streets was a popular place for all ages. It closed in 1964.

In the photo above a machine fastens paper hoods over the inner cap and rim of the milk bottle.

The milkman faithfully carried bottles in metal carriers to the householder's door, rain or shine, summer or winter.

John Nicholson established a printing company on the west side of North 9th Street which was known for some time as a local landmark. Nicholson was joined by his brother, Timothy, who came to Richmond from Haverford College, near Philadelphia. Timothy became president of Nicholson & Brother at 729 Main Street, dealing in books, stationery and wallpaper. He also was president of Nicholson Printing and Manufacturing, publishers, printers, bookbinders and paper-box manufacturers, located at 26-30 North 9th Street. Timothy served as a trustee of Earlham College for 19 years.

George W. Miller (1860-1929), a native of Connecticut, came to Wayne County with his parents at age five. He worked on a farm near the small town of Salisbury, then clerked in Irvin Reed's hardware store. In 1880 he formed a partnership with Charles H. Pogue and they moved their business from 9th and Main streets to the west side of Fort Wayne Avenue. George and his brothers, Fred and Jacob, joined in 1909 to form Miller Brothers Hardware.

Hotels

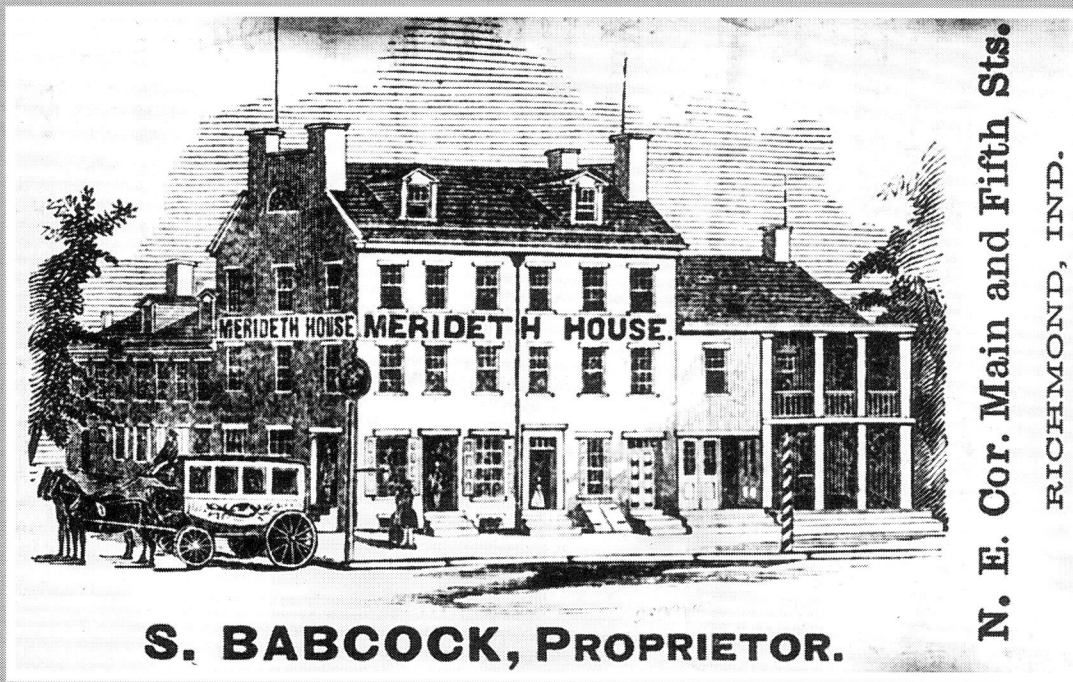

Meredith House at the northeast corner of Main and 5th streets, later renumbered as 8th Street, was managed in 1857 by Stephen Babcock and by Reuben Fuller in 1865. This later became the site of the Dickinson Trust Company. Either the sign painter or the artist transposed an *e* and an *i* in this drawing.

The hotel at 621 Main Street was early known as Githens House then as the Grand Hotel. George Klein was owner and manager from 1889 to 1923 when he leased it to his nephew, William T. Klein. The Grand catered to the many traveling salesmen who came through Richmond. Stephen O. Yates, a well-known Richmond architect, had his office on the second floor. The State Theater was later raised on this site.

The High Point Hotel occupied a spacious site at the west edge of Glen Miller Park. It was later found to be in a restricted area and was demolished in 1904. The Low Point Hotel, by contrast, was a saloon at the southeast corner of 23rd Street and East Main Street.

In 1894 about 50 Richmond men formed the Commercial Club, forerunner of today's Chamber of Commerce. Building the Westcott Hotel at the northeast corner of 10th and Main streets was their first major project. John M. Westcott, president of the Hoosier Drill Company, was a major stockholder in the project and later purchased the hotel. It was considered a fashionable address to rent an apartment or to visit.

The Arlington Hotel at 9th and North E streets, southeast corner, catered to the salesmen who arrived via the railroad, as well as actors in the local opera houses.

Among Richmond's 19th century hotels was the Phillips House, white building at far right, at 14-16 North 6th Street, owned by Abraham Phillips (1820-1884), born in Pennsylvania. City directories indicate it existed in the 1870s. Phillips traveled first to Macomb, Illinois, in 1836, then to Madison, Indiana, before settling in Richmond in 1838. He was a cabinetmaker and also made coffins, skills useful in any community. Phillips House was torn down in 1950.

Just south of Phillips House was a building, dark color with two gables, owned by Arthur Charles Lindemuth (1854-1939), like Phillips, born in Pennsylvania. He came to Richmond with his parents from Greenville, Ohio, in 1877 after graduating from Cornell University. He was a lawyer, judge, city attorney from 1888 to 1898 and served two terms in the state legislature. This building was razed for a parking lot.

Leland Hotel

The Richmond-Leland Hotel was formally opened September 15, 1928. Mayor Lawrence A. Handley was the featured speaker and 400 people attended a celebration dance.

The seven-story brick structure in a Spanish Colonial/Mission style stands on the northeast corner of South 9th and A streets. The former factory of the Richmond Casket Company had to be demolished to make room. A larger basement required removal of soil that was taken to the light plant site as fill.

The hotel ballroom was popular for formal dances, receptions, reunions. Many families celebrated Thanksgiving and other holidays by reserving tables in the dining room. Apartments on the top one or two floors were often leased to longtime residents. A one-story section to the north, removed in 1994, at one time held the Sears, Roebuck store along with other shops and the hotel garage.

In 1985 the hotel became a Radisson, part of the Radisson Hotel Corporation franchise. The hotel has been remodeled recently and is again open as the Leland and owned by Professional Planning Consultants, Inc., of Columbus, Ohio.

When the Leland Hotel was remodeled and reopened as the Radisson in 1986. Woody Herman and his Thundering Herd provided the dance music.

The City Market

The Richmond City Market at the southwest corner of 6th and South A streets was built parallel to A Street. Ample parking was provided for farm wagons of the vendors.

The market was built by John McMinn in 1855 (left). It has been replaced by the Saturday and Tuesday farmers market (below) on North E Street. The market building was declared unsuitable for repair and was torn down for a parking lot in 1956.

In 1908 the Atlantic & Pacific delivery wagon was a familiar sight as grocery orders were sent out from the store at 727 Main Street. Delivery boy Paul Witte, 14 years old, poses with his little friend, Paul Beall.

Fruits and vegetables were not wrapped in plastic, but purchasers could choose their potatoes, squash and ears of corn from the grocers' open bins.

Although a purchaser could select vegetables and fruit from open baskets, there was no reaching over the counter to pick up the canned items. The clerk performed that task in addition to grinding the fresh coffee.

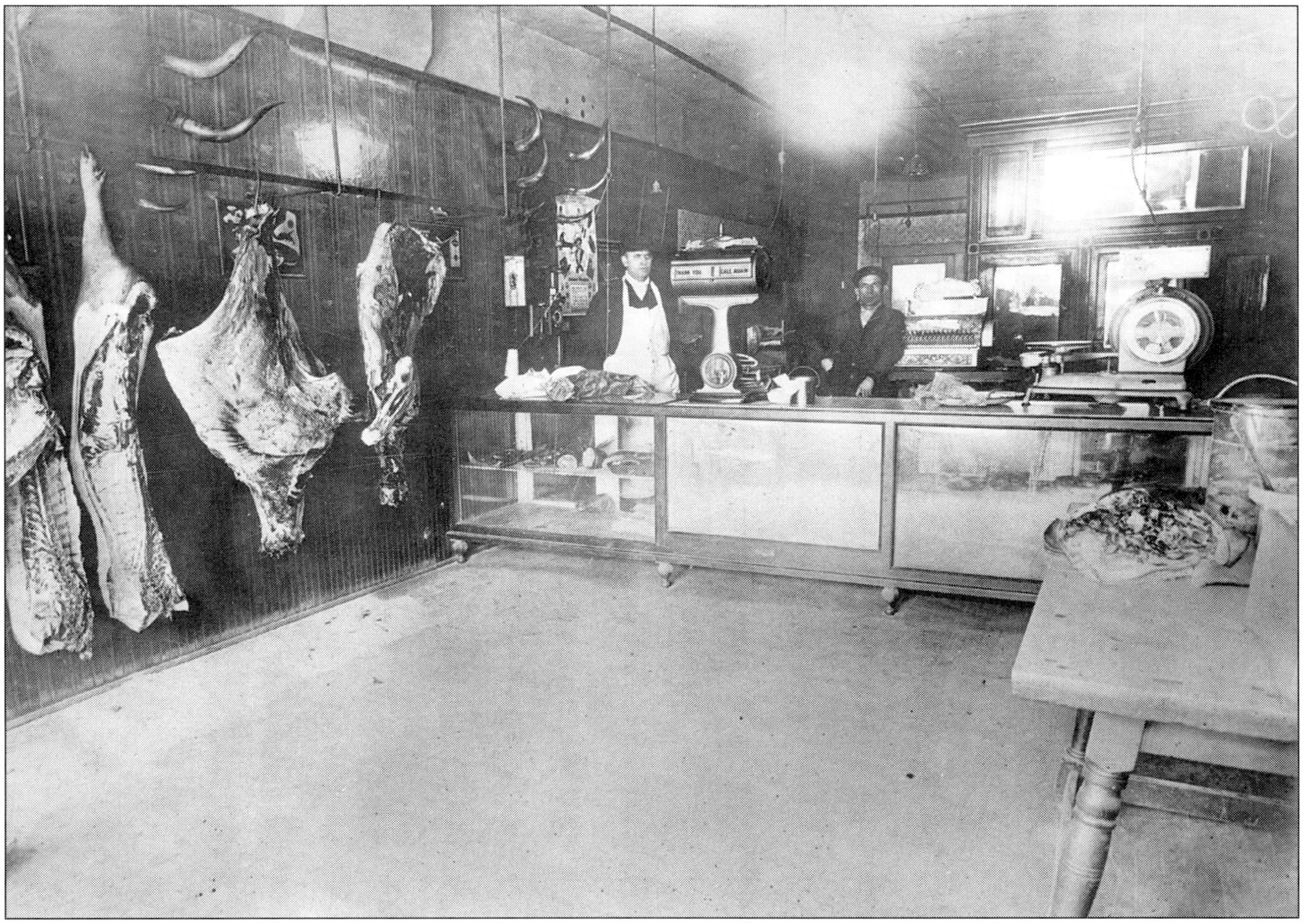

Government sanitary standards did not exist in this meat market. However the meat was fresh, and the buyer might have his meat cut to order.

Eggemeyer Grocery

Thomas Nestor established his grocery business in 1851 and also packed and shipped butter and eggs at North Washington Street. He took on John M. Eggemeyer (1850-1935) as a partner in 1878 and they set up shop at South 4th and Main streets. The 401 Main Street address served as the grocery store and on the north side of Main, at 402, was their egg and butter packing plant.

By the time the Eggemeyer store acquired a motorized delivery vehicle the firm had grown to encompass the luxury of four telephone numbers. During this period Thomas Nestor retired.

John M. Eggemeyer in 1892 built a large new store at 401-403 Main Street. With the grocery on the street level, there was additional income from apartments on the second and third floors.

Even though a home lacked the convenience of an electric refrigerator, with groceries within easy walking distance it was possible to have fresh vegetables, bread and meat every day. Henry and George Cutter's store was popular with the neighbors at South 4th and D streets. In 1857 it was the site of Frederick Landwehr's store until his new building was ready at South 7th and E streets. In 1893 John Hasecoster designed the commercial Romanesque style building for the Cutters with the older part of the building, at right, designated Ed Cutter's saloon. Cutter, Landwehr and Hasecoster all came from the Osnabrueck area, Kingdom of Hanover (Germany). Roland Hirschfeld, a clerk for the Cutters, bought the store in 1946. It is now the location of a craft shop.

At 217 South 5th Street an Italianate-style residence was remodeled to house the Kahle Brothers' neighborhood grocery.

The Kahle brothers, William and Joseph, and Tony Luerman, at center, prepared for the Christmas season with candy canes and other confections at the South 5th Street store.

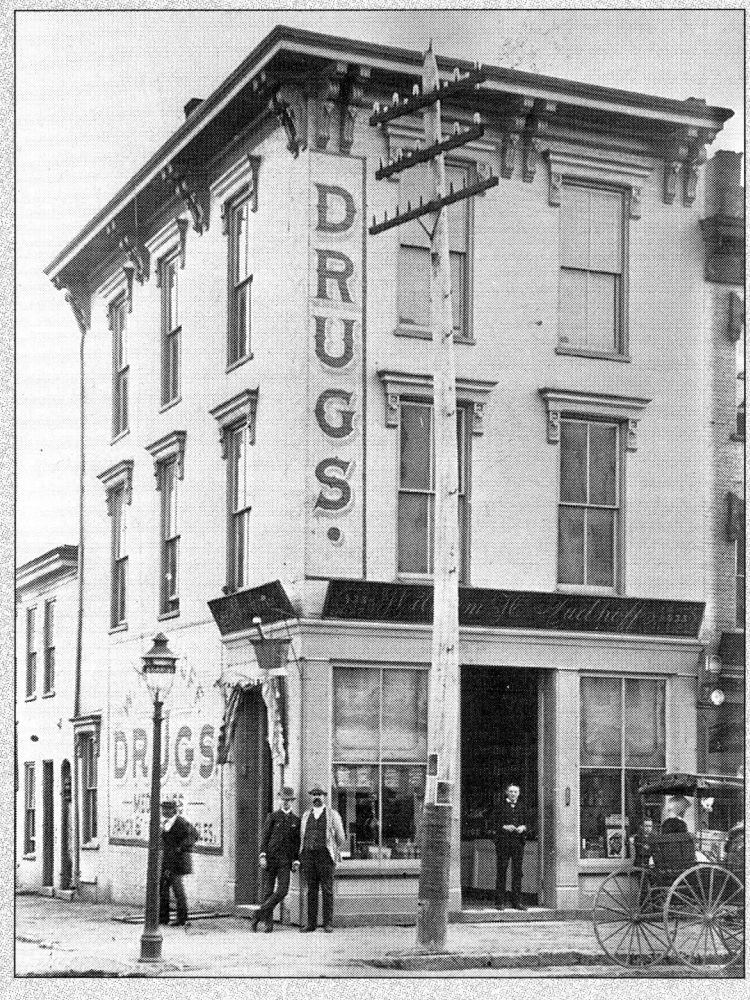

The drugstore of Gustave Sudhoff (1874-1939), located at 435 Main Street, was a nicely proportioned Italianate-style structure, although rather small for a three-story building. William (1855-1931), Gustave's son, was a druggist for 50 years. A two-seater surrey waits at the curb.

Horace L. Dickinson (1867-1943) and his large staff of well-dressed salespeople sold wallpaper at 504 Main Street.

The daily supply of ice in a large block is delivered to Lou's Sample Room where thirsty patrons could imbibe Emil Minck's lager beer, advertised in the two signs on the building. The man in the apron is probably the owner.

William B. Golden maintained his Club Cigar store at 406 North 8th Street. The building's unusual shape provided billboard space at the side.

James A. Hiatt's Drug Store at 419 North 8th Street sold a variety of products including freshly ground coffee, ice cream sodas and sundaes. Bentwood chairs and an Eastlake-style table were provided for customers. The ubiquitous spittoon is visible on the floor at the left.

John H. Cranor (1849-1918) and William D. Loehr (1868-1949) began their Main Street Clothiers in 1889. Cranor retired in 1894 because of ill health and John Klute was hired as a clerk. Klute had experience as a clerk at Nicholson's Book Store. Later the firm was known as Loehr & Klute, and then as Loehr's.

James S. Starr & Sons sold one-price clothing in their store on the site of a branch of the first state bank in Indiana, and several subsequent banks. Robert Morrisson is believed to have built the brick building. Part of it housed Plummer & Morrisson's pharmaceutical company.

George Fox & Son sold men's clothing at their store, 628 Main Street, founded in 1871 by Solomon Fox, father of George. They later moved to 706 Main Street.

Mrs. Augustus (Margaret Alice) Kielhorn's millinery shop at 525 Main Street provided chic chapeaux for the fashionable women of Richmond. The Kielhorns came to Richmond in 1895 from Cannelton, Indiana. They erected the three-story building on Main Street, and lived above the store until moving to a new house on the northwest corner of South 17th and A streets.

The attractive interior decor of Mrs. Kielhorn's shop featured the graceful vine on the light fixture and a variety of potted plants.

Mrs. Kielhorn, about 1895, wearing one of her stylish hats.

The flooding of the Whitewater River was responsible for bringing Richmond its first pharmacist. Irvin Reed (1809-1891) of Zanesville, Ohio, decided to make the city his home in May, 1833, when his four-horse stagecoach found the river impassable. In 1834 he married Mary M. Evans formerly of Baltimore. Reed changed over to the hardware business in 1857 on Main Street between 5th and 6th streets, then moved to 631 Main Street, now Phillips Drugs. Each of the Reed sons worked in the store until going on to other jobs. The youngest, Frank, entered the family business in 1876 after making a trip west, and remained until his death in 1933. The store closed in 1935.

Clara T. Moormann's shop at 520-522 Main Street stocked books, stationery, wallpaper and artists' materials at the turn of the century.

The interior view of Miss Moormann's shop included framed pictures, vases and candlesticks. Clara Moormann died in Florida in 1941.

Thomas W. Hayward (1832-1909) and his son, Jacob (1855-1940), moved their westside grocery into their new building at 96 West Main in 1902. It was directly west of Augustus Rodefeld's blacksmith shop. Jacob and his family lived in the spacious apartment over the grocery. In 1926 it became a restaurant owned by Robert Snavely, and from 1933 to 1939 it was called the College Inn. More recently it was the office of Dr. Paul Pentecost and then of Dr. Tom Ebbinghouse. The brick building was razed in 1993 by Rodefeld's Auto Parts.

In 1906 Walter J. Doan (1859-1939) and Edward H. Klute (1861-1937), undertakers, were located on South 8th Street, but moved in 1909 to 1106 Main Street. At this address a residence was remodeled to offer the funeral facilities on the first floor with a furnished apartment above for the Doan family.

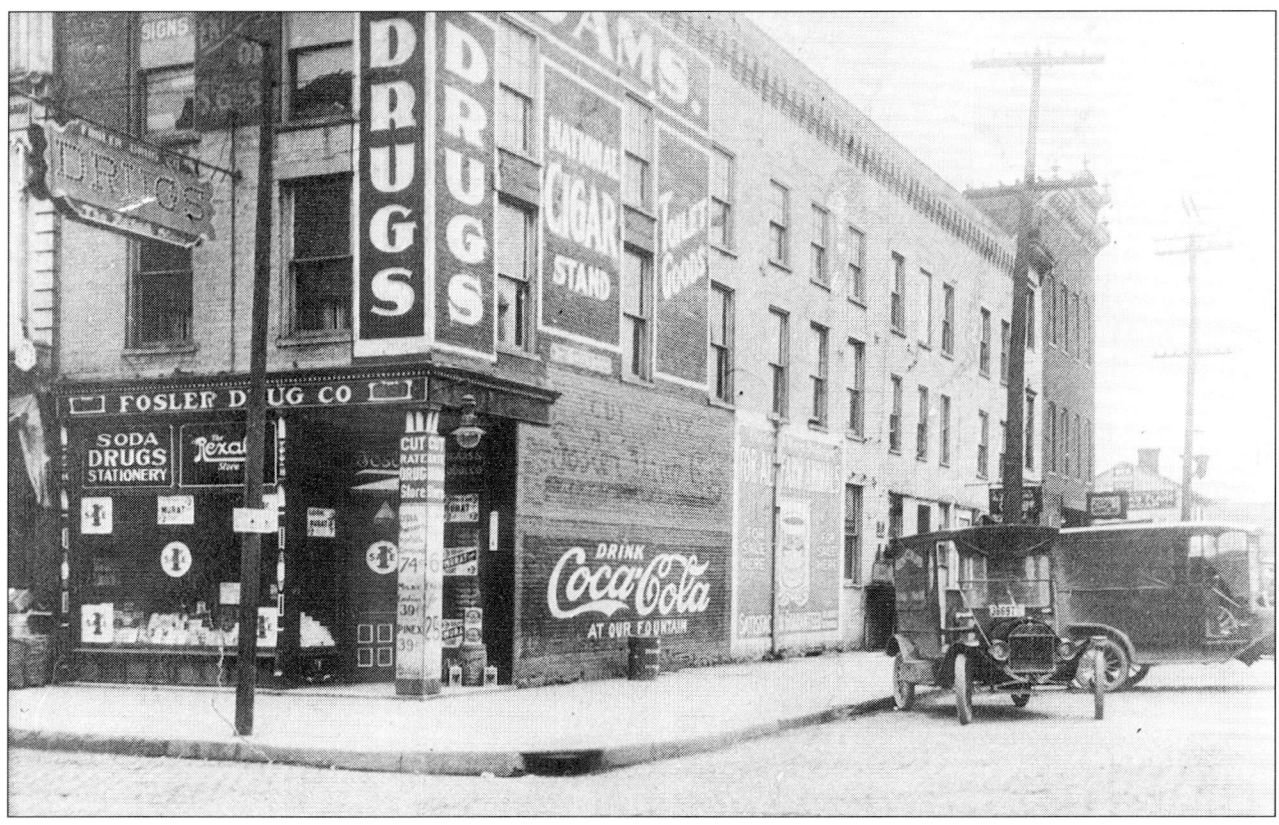

John Fosler (1880-1947), son of I. T. and Martha Dougan Fosler, graduated from Purdue's School of Pharmacy in 1902. He opened one drugstore in West Richmond in 1908 and a second one in 1914 at 601 Main Street, formerly Adams Drug Store.

John Fosler and his younger brother, Herbert (1889-1945), visit with customers in John's store which was decorated with a lamp and fancy shade at the soda fountain dispenser. The tin ceiling pictured was common in Richmond stores of that era. In 1925 John became head pharmacist at the Dayton, Ohio, Veterans Hospital.

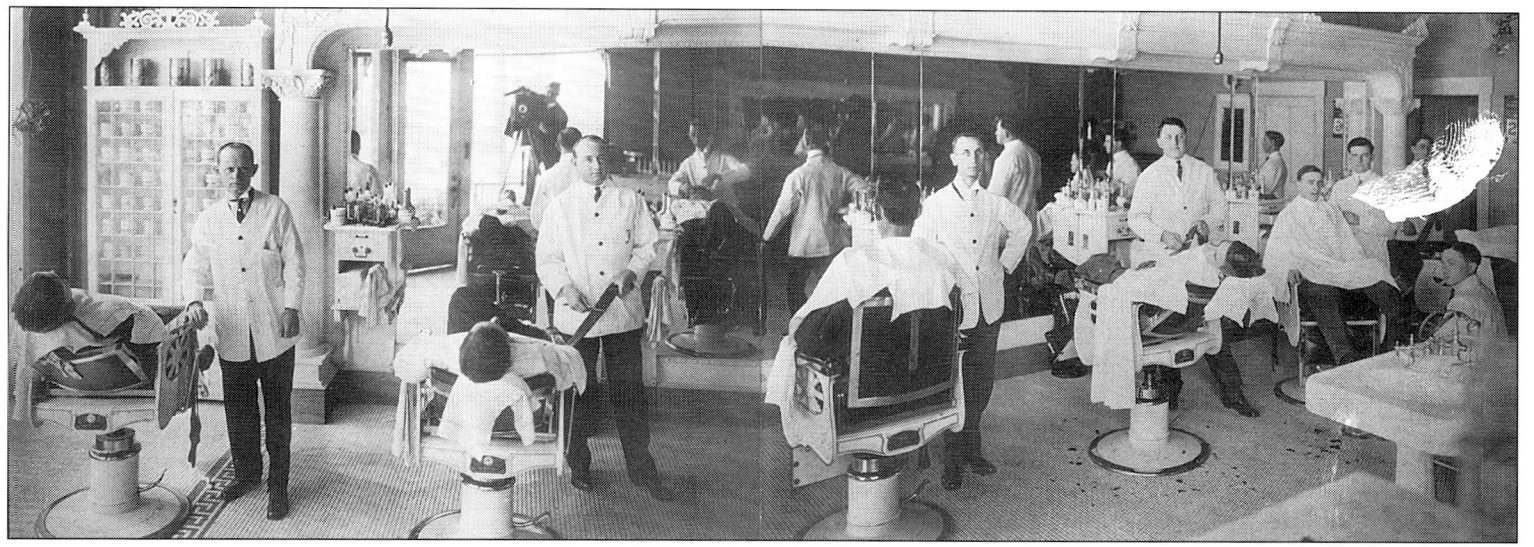

Elmer Harter, barber, ran a busy early-day 5-chair shop at 1001 Main. The mirrors were considered a stylish addition to the decor. Note that the barbers stored their customers' shaving mugs in a large cabinet, at left. One barber sharpens his straight razor on the leather strop.

Fort Wayne Avenue, part of the old Quaker Trace leading to Fort Wayne, met Main Street at North 4th Street with the Wayne Hotel on the west and Quigley's Drug Store on the northeast corner.

From 4th Street, Main Street slopes westward toward the bridge over the Whitewater River. The Wayne Hotel is visible at the right and small shops line the street westward to the Swayne, Robinson Company.

Shores dry goods store supplied customers on the east side of the city with notions and other inexpensive items at 1512 East Main Street.

Price's Confectionery sold their candy and ice cream at 916 Main Street. Eugene Price, pictured with three of his employees, waits for customers near his soda dispenser equipped with a light fixture. Hires Root Beer was also served and customers could take their "black cows" and other treats to the tables in the rear. Black and white tiles cover the floor. Eugene was a grandson of Charles T. Price Sr., a grocer, developer and realtor in Richmond. The confectionery business was started in the 1860s by Charles T. Price, Jr.

Elizabeth Parker's restaurant was in the brick building in the photo at the left before moving into the addition to the right. This 1616 East Main Street location is now called Taste o' the Town. Parker earlier ran a restaurant in Eaton, Ohio.

Bar-b-que was the specialty at 901 North H Street where Marzel Webster and his grandson, Bobby, ran Bar-B-Que Heaven.

Banking in Richmond

In the early days of Richmond, money was scarce and there was generally trading or bartering of one kind of product for another. To obtain salt for preserving food and pelts, families or friends would send a wagon-load of skins, maple sugar and farm products to Cincinnati for a load of salt. Land, however, had to be paid for with money.

As the community expanded and prospered, banks became a necessity. The first bank was a branch of the State Bank of Indiana, chartered in 1833. The Richmond branch started December 1, 1834, with Robert Morrisson as largest stockholder and Achilles Williams as president. Elijah Coffin, Quaker teacher and storekeeper, was chosen as cashier and he stayed with the bank until the expiration of its charter, January 1, 1859. The bank was on the northeast corner of 5th and Main streets.

When the former State Bank closed, the Richmond National Bank filled the gap, along with an affiliated bank called the Citizens' Bank. Their reserves were reported to be in the form of Spanish and Mexican dollars kept in kegs holding $20,000 each. The son of Elijah Coffin, Charles F. Coffin, and his son, Charles H. Coffin, were both associated with this bank. They seemed to have made unfortunate investments in western lands and the Richmond National Bank failed in 1884 causing a great panic.

The Second National Bank, started in 1872, came to the rescue of the failed Richmond National Bank by providing funds for the city, the schoolboard of Wayne County and county officials.

The Union National Bank was an outgrowth of the Centerville National Bank, reorganized and moved to Richmond in 1855. It occupied the former Richmond National Bank building at 5th and Main streets. In June of 1887, when the Kelly-Hutchinson building on the southeast corner of 8th and Main was completed, the bank moved to that location.

A later move was into the Hittle Building at the northwest corner of 9th and Main streets. John Hasecoster, Richmond architect, designed both the Kelly-Hutchinson and Hittle buildings.

The First National Bank at the northwest corner of 7th and Main was organized in 1863 and located at this site although in an earlier building. The structure shown here was built about 1880. The present building, a larger one in the same block, is occupied by Bank One.

This building was put up by Andrew Scott and was occupied by the Second National Bank, chartered in 1872, of which Scott was the president.

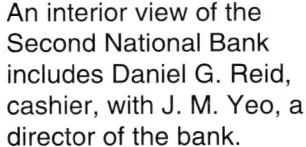

Seven employees of Second National Bank pose for the camera in front of the new entrance of Second National Bank.

An interior view of the Second National Bank includes Daniel G. Reid, cashier, with J. M. Yeo, a director of the bank.

Star Bank

Andrew Scott

When the Second National Bank opened for business on July 1, 1872, new gas lamps had just been installed on Main Street and citizens were looking forward to horse-drawn trolleys in 1873. Mark Twain was calling the period, "the gilded age."

The first officers of the bank were: Andrew F. Scott, president; John B. Dougan, cashier; James Thomas, treasurer. Its first balance sheet, October 3, 1872, showed deposits of $39,327.00 and total resources of $212,317.00.

In 1986, the Second National Bank was acquired by the First National Cincinnati Corporation and retained that name until July 1, 1988 when the corporation changed its name to the present Star Bank.

When, in 1972, the bank celebrated its 100-year anniversary F. Wayne Stidham was president. Today his son, David W. Stidham, serves in that position.

An interior view of the former Second National Bank shows its coffered ceiling.

The second building used by the Second National Bank was on the northwest corner of 8th and Main streets and is a handsome example of Classic Revival architecture. The facade is now covered with decorative metal and houses Harrington Bank.

Construction of Dickinson Trust Company in 1916 on the northeast corner of 8th and Main shows the Kelly-Hutchinson Building in the background.

The Dickinson Trust building before being remodeled in 1955 for the Second National Bank, now known as Star Bank. This is another example of Classic Revival architecture.

An excellent adaptive reuse of existing property is shown by the Italianate house converted to the eastside branch of Star Bank, at 2909 East Main Street.

RICHMOND, IND. MOTORCYCLE CLUB PICNIC

Chapter 4
Good Times in Richmond

Photo left: Bicycle racing was popular at the Driving Park on the east side of Richmond, now part of the Hayes Regional Arboretum. The mile track was designed by Robert A. Howard (1829-1910), civil engineer and Wayne County surveyor, also famous for laying out the Indianapolis Speedway. The track was equally well attended for horse racing. The group pictured on the track are members of the Henley Bicycle Manufacturing Company's racing team.

Photo below: The Richmond Motorcycle Club held its annual family picnic on September 26, 1915.

Entertainment in early Richmond was limited to work-related occasions such as corn huskings, barn raisings and quilting bees. Later the fun times centered around institutions like churches, schools, firehouses and even taverns. Membership in debating societies, fraternal organizations or ethnic groups such as the song fests of the Liederkranz or people's choirs. As bands developed parades were organized to commemorate almost any celebration.

In 1904 the Chautauqua provided a family occasion to enjoy the great outdoors in Glen Miller Park as well as enjoying stimulating intellectual programs, music and camaraderie. Horticultural and agricultural fairs were a time to enjoy games and picnics. The several opera houses brought traveling theatrical troupes and minstrel shows.

Then, too, we must not forget the hours spent singing around the Starr piano.

Rollin' in Richmond

There must be something about a wheel that appeals to nearly everyone, from hoop racers to yo-yo experts. Wheels become especially interesting when attached to one's feet in the form of roller skates or the more modern roller blades. A board with wheels and a handle, or a scooter, has been a favorite of many children.

In the 1890s Richmond's athletic young people took to their bicycles with enthusiasm. Newspaper reports tell of groups "Wheeling" to Hagerstown, Milton or even Hamilton, Ohio, for an outing. Perhaps the visitors would relax on someone's porch with a tall glass of lemonade before the return trip.

Soapbox derbies tested a young person's ingenuity, then along came motorcycles and the automobile.

Micajah C. Henley (1856-1927), a distinguished-looking gentleman, manufactured roller skates, bicycles, lawn mowers and wire fencing.

The Henley Rollabout, a type of scooter, was called "a new and novel outdoor and indoor vehicle for children of all ages." It was manufactured by the firm in 1913.

Pictured is the Henley residence at 201 North 14th Street. It was remodeled after Henley received a large order for roller skates from South America. The house is a variant of the Queen Anne style.

Stella Johnson Porter (1872-1947) makes a statement in this photo which announces that women, too, were attracted to the sport of bicycling. The lacing over the rear wheel prevented a woman's skirt from tangling in the spokes..

A group of cyclists and spectators gather in front of the Duersch cycle shop while on a trip to Hamilton, Ohio.

The Pavilion at Glen Miller Park provided a rest stop for cyclists and their friends.

W. H. Duning's bicycle shop supplied parts and equipment for the avid cyclist.

Bill Bradway (1874-1949) was an expert bicycle repairman and also held the record for Wayne County mile champion in 1898.

The Henley Company sponsored one of Richmond's roller polo teams. Members of the team in 1901 were photographed with M. C. Henley. In the front row, left to right, are Mace Beyer, Roscoe Stevens and Billy Patterson. In the back row appear Jeff Van Allen, Chauncey Fischer, Henley, and C. W. (Shorty) Jessup.

One of the contestants in the 1949 Soapbox Derby has his racer weighed before the event. The course was on North E. Street just west of Glen Miller Park.

Jimmy Brunton won the 1952 Richmond Optimist Club Soapbox Derby. Regional winners moved on to compete in Akron, Ohio. Jimmy's sister and mother look on as local club members present the trophy.

Museums of Richmond

While these two pages are concerned with the history of the Wayne County Historical Museum, Richmond and Wayne County are fortunate to have ten other museums spanning a wide range of interests. Some are devoted to specialized topics, such as the pottery and artwork of the Overbeck sisters of Cambridge City. The Indiana Football of Fame contains displays and information relating to that sport, and is housed in the former Richmond Post Office. The Richmond Art Museum at McGuire Hall has an excellent permanent collection and special exhibits.

The Levi Coffin house at Fountain City honors the man often called the president of the Underground Railroad, and the Huddleston Farmhouse Inn Museum does the same for a pioneer family on the National Road at Mount Auburn. An outdoor setting for the study of local trees is provided at the Stanley Hayes Regional Arboretum, and also offers summer classes.

The Mansion House at Centerville is a former carriage stop and tavern on the National Road. The Abram Gaar House shows what life was like for a prosperous family in Richmond in the 1870s. The Joseph Moore Museum of Earlham College displays facets of natural history, while the Hagerstown Museum covers that area's cultural history.

The current home of the Wayne County Historical Museum was originally the Hicksite Friends meeting house at 1150 North A Street. The structure was designed by George Hoover, an architect who came to Richmond from Pennsylvania.

Julia Meek Gaar (1859-1944), of an early Wayne County family, was the driving force behind the Wayne County Historical Museum, and acquired the former Hicksite Quaker meetinghouse to display artifacts collected during her worldwide travels. She and William Gaar were married in 1882. Standing behind her is their son, James Milton Gaar (1883-1945), who was a brigadier general in the U. S. Army. He retired, moved to Canada, and died there.

The interior of the Hicksite meetinghouse features austere benches used when the Friends group met. Often men and women sat separate from each other and entered and exited the facility by different doors.

The interior of the former meeting house was transformed into the Wayne County Historical Museum. The major exhibits are an Egyptian mummy, a Wooten desk, local inventions, and 19th century home furnishings.

The familiar bust of Buddha was purchased by Mrs. Gaar. Also on the grounds are original log houses and re-creations of a livery stable, bakery, and printing shops.

William J. Wedekind (1866-1926), a Hagerstown blacksmith and farrier, won a premium prize at the 1893 World's Columbian Exposition at Chicago with an exhibit of his work. It contains horseshoes (some for hoof defects), tools of his own design, his photograph and a blacksmith shop in miniature. He was offered $100,000 for the exhibit in its handsome wooden case, but he refused to sell. Wedekind's sister-in-law, Minnie Bunnell, at left, gave it to the Wayne County Historical Museum.

Gaar Williams' newspaper cartoons often contained Richmond-related items. At Richmond High School, he was staff artist for the *Argus*. He attended Earlham College in 1897.

Gaar Williams (1880-1935) studied at the Cincinnati Art Academy and the Chicago Art Institute. He was artist for the *Chicago Daily News*, political cartoonist for his cousin's, Rudolph Leeds', *Indianapolis News*, and then at the *Chicago Tribune* from 1921 to 1935.

Harry Frankel (1888-1948), known as Singin' Sam, the Barbasol Man, was one of the highest paid radio performers of the 1930s. After a career in New York, he and his wife, Smiles, retired to Richmond.

Polly Bergen, motion picture and television performer, lived in Richmond as a child and attended Starr Elementary School, Test Junior High School and Richmond High before the family moved to Compton, California. Her father, William Burgin, was a construction engineer and his work took them to several cities. At the age of 12, Polly sang on Radio Station WKBV.

Notables in Richmond History

The people featured on pages 96 to 101 represent some of the more well-known faces of Richmond's past. They form a contingent of artists, businessmen, performers and recorders of Richmond's history and heritage both through the medium of the written word as well as through the eyes of the camera lens.

Daniel Gray Reid (1858-1925) began his financial career as a messenger boy for Second National Bank, was promoted to cashier and then invested funds in a small tin-plate company at Elwood which burgeoned into the American Can Company. Reid, William B. Leeds and two partners took control in 1901 of the Rock Island Railroad. Reid remembered his hometown and made generous gifts to community organizations.

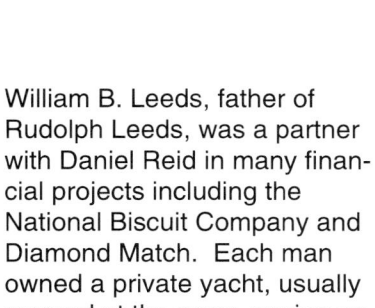

William B. Leeds, father of Rudolph Leeds, was a partner with Daniel Reid in many financial projects including the National Biscuit Company and Diamond Match. Each man owned a private yacht, usually moored at the same marina on the East Coast.

Edward Gurney Hill (1874-1933) and his sister, Sarah (1853-1930), started a greenhouse near their home on East Main Street in 1887 in order to grow roses as cut flowers. In 1881 their father, Joseph, with E. Gurney, started growing flowers on a small scale near 20th and East Main streets. Sarah became expert at the hybridizing process and many new varieties of roses were developed. After about 20 years of business growth, a new range of greenhouses was developed west of the city, near North West 18th Street, creating over 650,000 square feet of space. Some of their patented roses are Forever Yours, Coed, Jack Frost, Promise Me, and Royalty.

Henry Clay Fox (1836-1920) was born in Preble County, Ohio, and came to Centerville to study law with George Julian after attending Whitewater College in that town. He has been a lawyer, district attorney and judge of the Wayne Superior Court and the Circuit Court. His detailed *Memoirs of Wayne County* were published in 1912.

Edna Stubbs Cathell (1879-1955) is best remembered for the bouquets of roses she painted for the E. G. Hill Company's patent applications. Her mother, a china and miniature painter, was her first art instructor. Edna then went on to study under other artists.

John E. Bundy (1853-1933) taught art at Earlham College from 1887 to 1895 when he devoted himself entirely to painting. He is well known for the many landscapes he painted, and for his influence in founding the Art Association of Richmond.

John Bundy sketched the first toll house west of the Main Street bridge, on the National Road. The road had been turned over to the Wayne County Turnpike Company. The toll house was at the southeast corner of Abington Pike and National Road.

Andrew Young has left us with *The History of Wayne County* published in 1872, but modestly said very little about himself. He also authored *Science of Government, American Statesmen* and *National Economy*.

Luther Feeger (1883-1975) was the son of Rev. Albert J. Feeger, pastor of St. John's Lutheran Church. He became associate editor of the *Palladium-Item* and wrote many historical columns for the newspaper which have been a great help to historians and genealogists.

Ella Bond Johnston (1860-1951) is credited with founding the RIchmond Art Association which is now housed in McGuire Hall, part of the RIchmond Senior High School. She was the sister of a well-known Richmond physician, Dr. Charles Bond, and her husband was Dr. Melville Johnston.

Marcus Mote (1817-1898), a Quaker and native of Ohio, was a prolific artist and well-known for his portraits of local notables, his political cartoons and large conversation pieces. He opened the Richmond School of Design in 1865 which had an overall enrollment of 541 pupils, both men and women.

Roy Hirshburg (1893-1957), an outstanding photographer, won many awards recognizing his considerable talent. His studio was on Main Street. He died from a gunshot wound inflicted by a jealous woman.

Edwin Dalbey, right, established a furniture business at 533 Main Street, and he and his son, Walter, above, became photographers when a customer traded a large camera for a piece of furniture. In addition to commercial photography, they published two important pictorial histories of Richmond in 1896 and 1906.

Dr. Mary F. Thomas (1816-1888) a native of Maryland, was the wife of Dr. Owen Thomas. She studied medicine first with her husband, then, after sewing enough clothing for her husband and two boys for six months, she studied at Penn's Medical College for Women. During the Civil War she was asked by Governor O. P. Morton to treat Indiana soldiers in several Union hospitals. She advocated voting and property rights for women and edited the temperance journal, the *Lily*, begun by Amelia Bloomer. Dr. Thomas served as physician for the Home of the Friendless and was the first woman admitted to the Indiana Medical College. She died of dysentery in 1888.

Dulcinea Mason Jordan (1833-1895), author of *Rosemary's Leaves*, edited Fred Maag's newspaper, the *Independent*. She also named Col. John F. Miller's park as Miller's Glen.

Esther Cooper Kellner, born in Henry County in 1908, started writing as a child. She later edited a children's magazine, *Playmate*. Titles of some of her books are *Bride of Pilate*, *The Devil and Aunt Serena*, *Out of the Woods*, *Moonshine* and *Animals Come to my House*. Her book, *Death on a Sunny Street*, illustrates both chaos and compassion during a tragic gas explosion in Richmond in 1968.

C. Francis Jenkins, on the left, (1868-1934) proved to be one of Richmond's best known inventors in the field of motion pictures and television. Among his many patents is one for the cardboard milk container. His first motion picture projector was demonstrated to a few members of his family in 1894 in the Main Street apartment above Jenkin's jewelry store. A plaque on the building west of Harrington Bank honors the occasion. Jenkins, his wife and his brother, Will, are shown when Francis piloted his own plane to Richmond to receive an honorary degree from Earlham College.

Palladium-Item

Palladium is the name of a statue of Pallas Athena. She is the patroness of newspapers because she exemplifies truth and wisdom. This statue is located in the lobby of the *Palladium-Item*.

Isaac Jenkinson (1825-1911) founded the *Fort Wayne Gazette* in 1863 and purchased the *Palladium* with Martin Cullaton in 1875. He was the last surviving member of the Electoral College that chose Lincoln as president and was named by President Grant as U.S. Consul to Scotland. He was active in education, too, serving on the board of trustees of Indiana University for 35 years and on the first board of trustees for Purdue.

Richmond has a history of multiple newspapers, perhaps reflecting a highly literate and informed populace. There were even two German language papers, the *Hausfreund* and Richmond *Volkszeitung*, but very few copies of these have survived. Not the earliest, but certainly the longest lasting, is the *Palladium-Item*.

The newspaper was organized on January 1, 1831, as the *Richmond Palladium* by Nelson Boon, great nephew of Daniel Boone. After six months the paper was sold to Thomas J. Larsh. David Holloway bought it in 1833, and barring a short break when it was owned by John Finley, kept an interest in it until 1875.

Isaac Jenkinson and Martin Cullaton, a printer, purchased the *Palladium* that year, and Jenkinson engaged several partners, including William Dudley Foulke, until he sold it in 1896. In 1906 Mrs. Jeanette Gaar Leeds acquired ownership and turned it over to her son, Rudolph G. Leeds. The *Palladium* and *Sun Telegram* merged in 1907.

Edward H. Harris, Sr., became co-editor and co-publisher along with R. G. Leeds in 1911. Luther M. Feeger was named managing editor in 1912.

Following the elder Harris' death in 1937, his role in the Palladium Publishing Company was taken over by his son, Edward H. Harris, Jr., and Luther Feeger assumed the role of business manager. Two years later another early paper, the *Item*, was added and the paper was renamed the *Palladium-Item and Sun-Telegram*, shortened in 1972 to *Palladium-Item*.

After the deaths of Mrs. Jeanette Leeds (1940), R. G. Leeds (1964), Edward H. Harris, Jr., (1969), and Luther Feeger (1975), the daily was sold to Gannett Newspapers, Inc., in 1976. The new company retained Edward S. Harris as editor and publisher for a year. The present staff is headed by Emmett Smelser, publisher, with Evan Miller as managing editor.

An early office of the *Palladium* newspaper at 920 Main Street. the firm also printed stationery, invoices and official forms.

In the arena of politics during the 1920s and 1930s the paper clearly opposed the Ku Klux Klan and asked for a grand jury probe into the state Republican Party's relationship with the Klan.

In 1956 the employees of the Palladium Publishing Company hosted a party at Forest Hills Country Club in honor of the 50th anniversary of Rudolph Leeds as editor, publisher and co-publisher. Left to right are Mrs. Horace Parker, Horace Parker, in charge of production of the newspaper; Florence Smith Leeds, Rudolph G. Leeds, Mrs. Edward Harris, Sr., widow of a former publisher; Luther Feeger, associate editor; Ed Harris, Jr., co-publisher, and Mrs. Ed Harris, Jr.

Linotype machines set hot type for the *Palladium-Item* at its North 9th Street building for many years before they were displaced by more modern methods.

The current home of the *Palladium-Item* is a contemporary Cubistic style facility at 1175 North A Street.

An almost idyllic setting for a Sunday afternoon, Richmond residents enjoy boating at Glen Miller Park. It appears that wearing a hat for both men and women was in vogue.

Richmond has been enriched by access to beautiful and well-maintained public parks. These green spaces are used for relaxation, meditation, family picnics, group activities and just plain fun.

In addition to Glen Miller, the South Tenth Street Park was one of the early Richmond green spaces. Swicker Park at South 7th and E streets was a public cemetery. In the 1880s the bodies were re-interred at Earlham Cemetery.

Freeman Park near Chester Boulevard, formerly named Shinkle, is currently home to the BMX Races.

Stanley W. Hayes (1865-1963) brought his factory that made railroad safety equipment from Geneva, New York, to Richmond in 1911. His sincere interest in trees and the natural world led to the formation of Hayes Regional Arboretum, a 355-acre site at 801 Elks Road. His desire to plant native trees was aided by advice from Charles Deam of Bluffton, Indiana, author of *Trees of Indiana*, and scientists from Earlham College. The arboretum is open to the public.

Col. John F. Miller (1830-1916) sold part of his extensive land holdings to Richmond for a park in 1885. The price was $35,000 to be paid in seven annual installments of $5,000 each. Miller was born at Ithaca, New York, worked for the New York Central Railroad, the Baltimore & Ohio, and then the Pennsylvania line. He was automatically retired at the age of 70 years.

Gardeners plant bushes at the E. G. Hill Memorial Rose Garden at Glen Miller Park. In 1985 a Rose Garden Project Committee was formed to expand the garden. This currently includes an All-American Rose Selection area and a Richmond Zweibrucken Friendship Garden.

Orrin Draver's swimming pool, 1520-22 Main Street, opened in 1922, and was called the best-equipped pool in the state. It was a favorite spot for local people including William Dudley Foulke (1848-1945), a lawyer, member of the State Senate and Chairman of the National Civil Service Reform League from 1888-1890. He was appointed in 1901 by President Theodore Roosevelt to the National Civil Service Commission. Foulke enjoyed swimming and convinced Draver to keep the pool open into October. Shown here are, left to right, Maureen, Foulke, Dot, Flo and Collins. In 1940 the building became a roller skating rink.

Many residents enjoyed sunning themselves on the sandy beach at Springwood Lake, now called Conservation Park, near Thistlethwaite Falls.

South 10th Street Park was originally laid out by William Bickle and John Laws for the people who owned property around it. It has been said that the first trees were planted to form the word "centennial." (It is not known if the park opened in 1876 or the developers hoped the trees would last 100 years.) Star brick of 1890 vintage was installed for a walk by Cecil Beard and Glen Barker in 1988 in the photo at left.

The teacher at the right is Dr. William Biddle, director of the Community Dynamics Program of Earlham College. He is shown in the 1950s, working with young people at Shinkle, later Freeman, Park. This park in the north part of the city is often used for bicycle races.

The Chautauqua was a Christian educational organization that visited many communities each summer for a week of intensive programming. It started in Richmond in 1904 and was held at Glen Miller Park. A note from the *Richmond Sun-Telegram* of August 24, 1906 read: "H.M. Crawford, manager of Keen's Outing Cottage Company is occupying one of their bug-proof, rain-proof and excellently ventilated cottages. It is worth examining. Everybody seems to be comfortably located in their tent homes. Many are preparing their meals while others patronize the dining tent."

CHAUTAUQUA

The Commercial Club, forerunner of the Chamber of Commerce, manned a tent.

In the entertainment-oriented world of today it is difficult to imagine life without radio, motion pictures or television. With increased leisure time there also was an interest in self-improvement through study and cultural pursuits. In 1847 a program was started in an attractive rural setting near Lake Chautauqua in western New York State by Dr. John H. Vincent and Lewis Miller to meet this need.

They offered a combination of classes and conferences lightened by outdoor recreation, singing and acting. Courses were given credit through New York and Syracuse universities. Ten days in August were set aside for the Chautauqua program.

In the early 1900s traveling Chautauquas extended into many tent-sites throughout the nation. The Chautauqua came to Richmond in 1904, affording a pleasant change of pace for entire families.

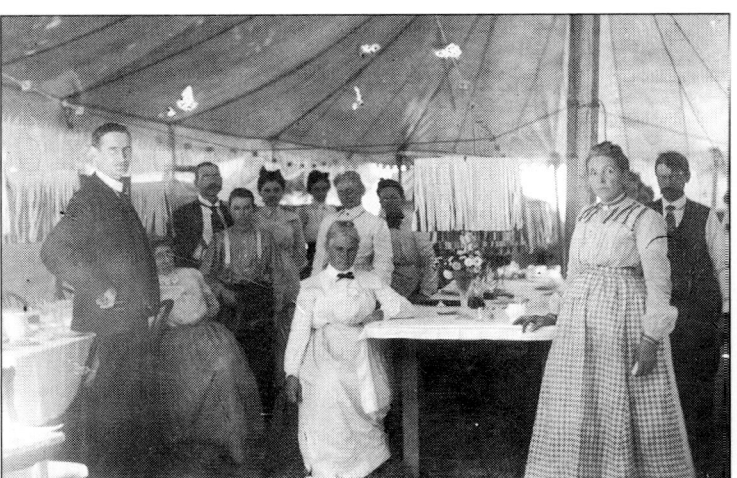

The dining tent was equipped with Windsor-type side chairs, a floral bouquet and fly whisks.

Ex-president Benjamin Harrison (1833-1901), seated at left, appeared in Richmond in April of 1895 to plant a tree in Glen Miller Park for Arbor Day. Other officials accompanied him in the barouche.

Ex-president Herbert Hoover (1874-1964), Lou Henry Hoover and their son, Allan, visited Earlham College in 1939 where Hoover was the commencement speaker and recipient of an honorary degree from the college. Herbert Hoover is related to the Hoover family of early settlers that came to this area from West Milton, Ohio.

Notable Visitors

David W. Dennis, assistant minority leader in the U.S. House of Representatives, conversed in 1969 with Representative Gerald Ford of Michigan. Dennis continues to practice law in Richmond.

Omar Murray opened his theater at 1007 Main Street in 1909. Today it is the home of Richmond Civic Theater, one of the area's cultural assets.

A popular motion picture theater, the State, opened in 1941 on the site of the former Grand Hotel, 619 Main Street. Robert Hudson, Sr., was proprietor.

Richmond Theaters

The Ritz Theater, built in the popular Spanish style, was later remodeled for Osco drugstore at 814 Main Street. Presently it is home to several community organizations as a meeting place.

The Tivoli Theater was the newest and largest movie theater in Richmond when it opened in 1926. The organ, a three-manual Wurlitzer with a wide range of orchestral instruments, was usually played by Ted Bock. This is at the northeast corner of 9th St. and Promenade.

People line up to purchase tickets for the opening of the State Theater in May 1941. The theater was destroyed in the downtown gas explosion of 1968.

111

A street acrobat attracted a crowd of anxious onlookers as he performed on the top level of the First National Bank at the northwest corner of 7th and Main streets.

A group of 13 touring cars line up across North A Street to celebrate Richmond as the Panic Proof City—called Panic Proof because the banks remained open during a financial panic in 1907. Although there are 13 autos, Number 13 was not awarded. Was someone superstitious?

Mr. and Mrs. Jones and family of North 15th Street decorated their touring car for a drive to Cambridge City to celebrate the 4th of July in 1905.

The crowd gathers for a performance at the Free Fair circa 1915.

The owner of a 1956 or '57 Dodge proudly displays his tail-finned beauty during Richmond Days on Main Street. The Kresge store is now John's Custom Framing, 823 Promenade.

Edward Y. Teas (1829-1918), born in Union County, attended Spiceland Academy and Earlham College. He and his brother, John, purchased a plant nursery at Indianapolis in 1852. In 1864, Edward and another brother, Thomas, bought John Conley's Richmond Nursery at South 5th and E streets and renamed it Cascade Nursery. E. G. Hill, the rose grower, credited Teas with helping him learn the nursery business. Teas also ran nurseries at Dunreith and Centerville. He helped organize the Indiana Horticultural Society in 1860.

"Popcorn Charlie" Hammond sold his specialty in 1894 at 8th and Main streets opposite the Kelly-Hutchinson building. Samuel Lewis, an expressman, waits in his wagon.

Richmond has always loved a parade. This circa 1895 photo, complete with horses and wagons, is shown at 9th and Main streets.

This 1937 parade passing by Knollenberg's and Vigran's features WW1 veterans and the high school marching band tailed by a trolley car.

The house of David Hoerner, the baker, on South 4th Street, became lodge hall for the Druids of Grove No. 29. This handsome late Italianate home shows the cornice brackets characteristic of the style and also has metal window-caps. Unfortunately, the edifice was demolished by Wayne County in 1978.

Fraternal Orders

The Elks Club purchased the home of Mrs. John Milton Gaar on North 8th Street. The residence had been designed by one of Indiana's best known architects, Francis Costigan (1810-1865), in 1858 for John Bridgland. Bridgland, a native of Virginia, was a successful businessman who was later appointed U. S. consul at LeHavre. The architecture is transitional between Greek Revival and Italianate. The home was razed to make way for a parking lot by Second National Bank.

This handsome Italianate building at the southwest corner of 8th and Main streets was erected in 1868 by the Independent Order of Odd Fellows. It now houses several businesses and offices.

One of the locations of the Masonic Lodge was this Romanesque-inspired building at the southeast corner of 9th and North A streets. It was demolished to make room for a Richmond Telephone Company building.

Originally designed for the First Presbyterian Church, this building ignited when the steeple was hit by lightning in 1885. It was remodeled by the Knights of Pythias as their lodge, on the east side of South 8th Street. The style is eclectic, a mixture of Italianate and French Second Empire. A new First Presbyterian Church was constructed at the northwest corner of 10th and North A streets.

The William G. Scott residence, erected in the 1860s at 204 North 10th Street, is an indeterminate style, sometimes called Queen Anne or Chateauesque. The red brick was imported and details are of brownstone and terra cotta. It was sold in the 1920s to the Knights of Columbus by Rhea Topping, Daniel G. Reid's daughter.

Music in Richmond

When the first Quakers came upon this part of Indiana, probably the only music they heard was from the song birds. The early Friends favored contemplative silence in their meetinghouses, not music.

The settlers from the duchies and principalities that were later united as Germany knew music in both vocal and instrumental form. Although many composers and musicians were supported by nobility, the hymns and choral music filtered down to the church-going population. They brought these hymns, songs and even instruments to their new homes, to the Lutheran and Catholic churches.

By 1863, for example, St. Andrew's Church in Richmond had Nicholas Collett as its organist. He was a native of Trier, Germany, a city on the Moselle River, where he had studied music.

The settlers from the southern states were familiar with music from dances, balls and other entertainments so when Charles Dickinson and John Popp opened a music store in town it was well frequented.

In 1847 a men's singing group, the *Liederkranz*, was started in New York City. By 1859 John Popp was named Grand Marshall at Richmond's Beethoven Liederkranz Society and their parade was headed by the city's Cornet Band. Following a picnic for the event, there was a ball at Starr Hall at the northeast corner of 8th and Main streets. The society's parade and picnic in 1867 included sack races and eating *smear kase* (cottage cheese) blindfolded.

The society celebrated the 100th birthday of Alexander Humboldt, German scientist and explorer, with a concert of vocal and instrumental music in 1869. The Cornet Band was just one of many in Richmond. The piano, invented by Bartolomeo Cristofori in 1709, was appreciated by most hearers for its wide range of sounds. Though not as portable as a violin or flute, it made a marvelous accompaniment for vocalists and for other instruments. Perhaps it was only natural that Richmond would become the site for a piano manufacturer, the Trayser Piano Company.

George Trayser, Alsatian by birth, had built pianos in Germany, Indianapolis and Hamilton, Ohio, then found extra financial support from Richard Jackson and James Starr in Richmond in 1872. In addition to investors, Richmond offered talented machinists and woodworkers.

After six years the company reorganized as the Chase Piano Company including M. J. Chase, a former associate of Trayser's, James Starr and Benjamin Starr. Jackson died in 1881 and the company was renamed James Starr & Company. Another change was in location as it moved from a downtown building to the Whitewater River Valley,

Plummer's 1857 City Directory shows the ad for Dickinson & Popp's Music Store. John Popp opened their music store at 35 Main Street about 1856. Pianos and other musical instruments were advertised in 1857 plus sheet music and instruction books. Popp was born in Bavaria in 1829 and came to Richmond in 1855. Dickinson's family had come earlier.

Mr and Mrs. G. M. Cole sold pianos and organs and gave lessons to aspiring Richmond musicians. Earlham students in particular were encouraged to take lessons which was surprising since Quakers generally discouraged the "frivolity" of music.

using the river as a power source. Jobs were provided for about 150 workers.

A major sales outlet for Starr pianos was the Jesse French Piano and Organ Company of St. Louis. Jesse French's father-in-law was John Lumsden of Nashville, Tennessee, and when Henry Gennett of Nashville married Alice Lumsden, John's daughter, he became involved in the piano industry, as well. In 1893 Henry Gennett and John Lumsden bought half ownership in the Starr Piano Company.

In spite of a fire at the factory and a flood in the valley, the company prospered and expanded. James Starr died in 1900 and Benjamin in 1903. At that time Henry Gennett took over the reins of the company, with help from his three sons. Harry was vice-president, Clarence, treasurer, and Fred, secretary. By 1915, they employed about 750 dedicated workers involved in all stages of piano making

In addition to conventional pianos, Starr began manufacturing the popular player piano in 1906. Practically all the parts for all their pianos were produced at the Starr factory complex. The exceptions were large castings made at Swayne, Robinson & Company at 3rd and Main streets. Phonographs gradually entered the market and the Starr company was able to compete in this market, too. This led to the development of pressing records at the Richmond plant and recording at a studio in New York City as well as in the Whitewater Valley.

Gennett Records included a wide range of music from vocalists to symphony orchestras to small bands, to speeches by William Jennings Bryan complete with sound effects, including railroad trains in Richmond. With the increasing popularity of radio, the Starr Piano Company output was reduced and the company was sold in 1952.

Gennett Records, however, over the expanse of its history, was to set records due to the increased popularity of jazz music. The recording studio was open on short notice to performers such as Hoagy Carmichael and Gene Autry.

Dissension in the family after the death of Harry Jr. caused the demise of Gennett Records in 1952.

A patriotic band was formed in Richmond at the time of the Civil War. It consisted of trombones, cornets and two kinds of drums. Musicians often formed a part of a regiment during this era.

The Richmond Independent Band played regularly in parades and for other civic events in the Richmond of 1910. Richmond's band history dates back to pre-Civil War days when bands performed and were applauded at fairs, park concerts, dances and opera house events.

Pictured is the Odd Fellows Whitewater Lodge Orchestra of 1920. Popularly played during this jazz era were slide trom bones, a bass drum, cymbals, trumpets, bass viol and clarinet. Most men's societies established their own bands and orchestras to play for their degree (or lodge achievement) work, as well as for parades and dances.

Many who knew violin maker, Alvin B. Clark, 1822-1911, predicted that his work could one day rival that of Stradivarius. Famous violinists patronized Clark's shop to have their violins repaired, to trade or to purchase a new instrument. At age 15, Clark produced his first violin while still living with his parents on a farm in New York. He came to Richmond a few years later, dying in the city at age 87. His last violin was made when he was 86 years old.

At one time Clark lived on South 8th Street. Later he moved with his wife to North 9th Street. After her death he moved to several small rooms on South 5th Street refusing money or offers of help. A benefit concert was planned for the aged master shortly before his death. The maestro, however, idolizing William Jennings Bryan, in weakened strength attended Bryan's chautauqua appearance. He contracted pneumonia and died two weeks later. His remains were sent to another city but his influence on the musical life of Richmond and those who place a high value on his workmanship lives on.

A. B. Clark as he sits in front of his shop at 430 Main Street.

The Elks' Boys' Band stands on church steps before a performance in 1941. Promoted and supported by the fraternal order, it was hoped that the sons would one day follow in their father's footsteps, join the order and eventually become a welcome addition to the men's band.

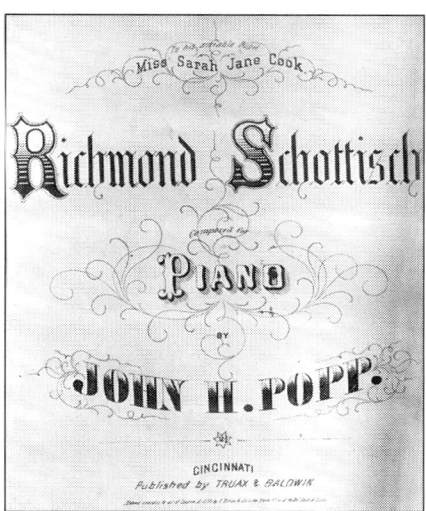

John Popp, one of the proprietors of Dickinson and Popp's Music Store, wrote the *Richmond Schottisch*, a piano composition for his student, Miss Sarah Jane Cook. The inscription reads "to my amiable pupil." Even during this era it was unusual for a teacher to dedicate a composition to a favored student.

Mr. and Mrs. Charles Kolp had a professional vaudeville dance troupe and toured throughout eastern United States. The couple eventually settled in Richmond at 326 North 10th Street. Gertrude Kolp (above) and her daughter, Elizabeth, taught dance to aspiring artists in their imposing residence, now known as High Tower.

The Richmond High School Red Devil Marching Band prepares for a competition or performance in this circa 1950 photo. Today's dynamic high school marching band and symphonic band are built upon an illustrious tradition of Richmond band history. This tradition dates back to pre-Civil War days when Richmond bands first played at theatres, dances and in all local parades.

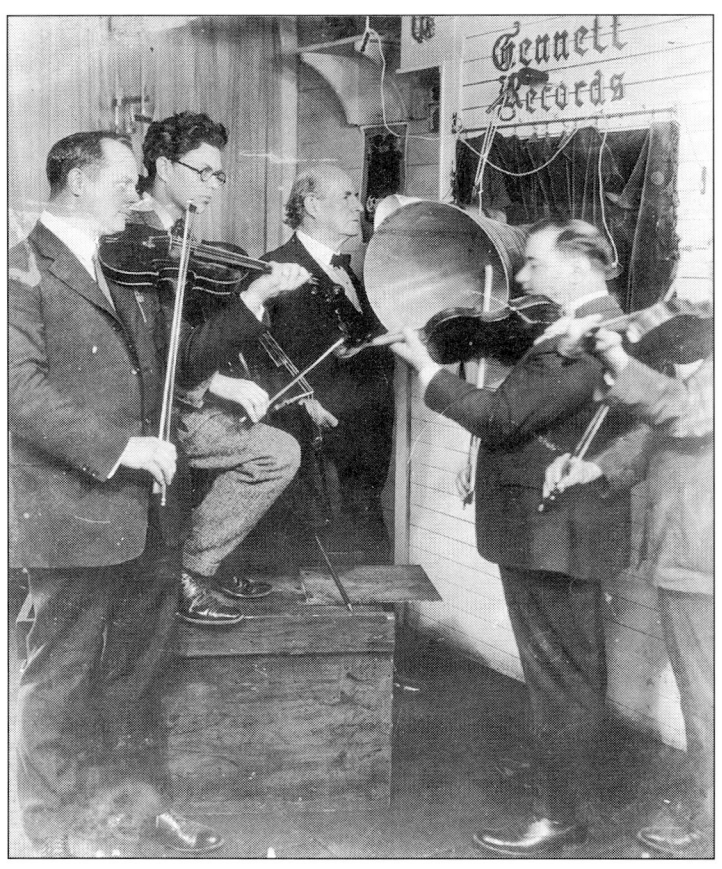

Clarence Gennett (1879-1953), middle son of Henry Gennett, served as treasurer of Starr Piano Company. The family, originally from Italy, with the name once spelled Gennetti, came to Richmond from Nashville, Tennessee.

Gennett Records, a branch of Starr Piano, on July 3, 1923 recorded William Jenning Bryan's famous "Cross of Gold" speech. The orator spoke against the gold standard in this speech given at the 1896 National Democratic Convention. The studio also recorded the 23rd Psalm with instrumental accompaniment.

A jazz band records at a soundproof Gennett Studio. The technician placed the instruments at various distances from the microphones according to the intensity of the instrument. Hence, the band's backs are to the camera. Pictured above is a Gennett Record label.

Professor Ben B. Custer (1825-1903) was born in Connersville, Indiana. His father was a cousin of General George Custer. Young Ben paid for private violin lessons for himself by performing odd jobs around town. He bought his favorite violin at a pawn shop for $15. He later discovered that the original owner had paid $600 for the instrument. From 1875-1898, after achieving state-wide renown, he gave lessons in Richmond. In 1889 Custer published a book entitled *50 Years in the Ballroom* which features a large selection of Custer's own dance music. He played for Abraham Lincoln in Bloomington, Illinois in 1859. His home in Centerville still stands in 1994.

"Joe" (Joseph Edgar) Maddy (1891-1966) supervised music in Richmond schools in the early 1920s. In a few short years he had organized "A" and "B" orchestras at every scholastic level, inspired an eight-member harp ensemble and established the first full symphony orchestra in a high school in the United States.

Joe Maddy astonished musical America when his young Richmond High School Symphony accompanied Pablo Casals at a national convention in Cincinnati, Ohio.

Drawing upon his years in Richmond, Dr. Maddy founded the internationally acclaimed National Music Camp and Arts Academy at Interlochen, Michigan.

Joe Longstreth won national and international recognition as a harpist, touring the U.S., Canada and Mexico for 16 years. He became widely known nationally as literary agent for convicted and executed killer and novelist Caryl Chessman. His regional fame, in Indiana, Ohio and Kentucky, came as host of radio and television shows in Dayton and Cincinnati. Born June 3, 1920, his life's experiences have been as varied as they are extraordinary - as a World War II pilot; as a resident of London, Paris, Rome and New York while an actor on stage, film and television productions. He has also taught English in European capitals and wrote children's books and an opera libretto. *Greg Pyle photo.*

Al Cobine, a Richmond product, is a modern jazz musician who started his own band at Indiana University and went on to play for jazz festivals throughout the Midwest. Occasionally he comes home to entertain his fans in Richmond.

Chapter 5: Governing Richmond

MAYORS OF RICHMOND.

1. John Sailor, 1840-1851.
2. John Finley, 1852-1866.
3. Lewis D. Stubbs, 1867.
4. Thomas N. Young, 1867-1868.
5. Thomas W. Bennett, 1869-1870, 1877-1883, 1885-1887.
6. James M. Poe, 1871-1872.
7. James Elder, 1873-1874.
8. James F. Hibberd, 1875-1876.
9. John L. Rupe, 1883-1884.
10. James W. Moore, 1887-1889.
11. John P. Thistlethwaite, 1889-1891.
12. Perry J. Freeman, 1891-1894.
13. James Ostrander, 1895-1897.
14. William W. Zimmerman, 1898-1905, 1910-1913, 1918-1921.
15. Richard Schillinger, 1906-1909.
16. Will J. Robbins, 1914-1917.
17. Lawrence A. Handley, 1922-1929.
18. Windsor B. Harris, 1930-1934.
19. Joseph M. Waltermann, 1935-1938.
20. John R. Britten, 1939-1947.
21. Lester E. Meadows, 1948-1955.
22. Roland H. Cutter, 1956-1963.
23. Edward Cordell, 1964-1967.
24. Byron Klute, 1968-1975.
25. Charles A. Howell, 1975.
26. Clifford J. Dickman, 1976-1983.
27. Frank Waltermann, 1984-1991.
28. Roger Cornett, 1992-

Underground Railroad

Wade Curry, shown in 1911, was a former slave given his freedom by Harold Reynolds of Fountain City, formerly called Newport, about nine miles north of Richmond.

The home of Levi and Catharine Coffin at Fountain City is reported to be where Eliza of Harriet Beecher Stowe's book, *Uncle Tom's Cabin,* was sheltered on her trip north. At least 2,000 fugitives were aided by the Coffin family or other Quakers in the vicinity. Levi Coffin was called the "president" of the Underground Railroad.

The Samuel Charles farmhouse east of the city at a site now included in Glen Miller Park was a "safe house" in the underground network. The E. G. Hill Memorial Rose Garden is directly south of the restored late Federal style house.

James M. Townsend (1843-1913) served as a minister at the Bethel African Methodist Episcopal Church and lived at 516 South 9th Street. Townsend Community Center in the north part of Richmond is named for him.

Courthouse

Being designated the county seat is an advantage to any community. The lawyers gather there, printers benefit from the official documents required, restaurants are full and local citizens are employed in various offices.

In southeastern Indiana a large county, Dearborn, was set up with Lawrenceburg as the county seat. As the population increased with the influx of settlers Wayne County was organized in 1810 and a new town named Salisbury was established as the county seat in 1811. The town, close to the Greenville Treaty Line, had William Commons raise a log courthouse. Lots were laid out and the town prospered.

A more permanent courthouse was needed so brickmasons from Ohio were hired. The old log courthouse was sold, moved to Richmond where it was placed on North 5th Street, covered with siding and used as a dwelling.

Meanwhile the route for the all-important National Road or Cumberland Road was laid out about one-third of a mile north of Salisbury, by-passing the county seat but going through Centerville, platted in 1814. There was great excitement among Centerville citizens to usurp the seat of county government.

The change was approved by the state and Centerville quickly designated a structure as a courthouse until a new one could be built in 1817, again by William Commons.

The 1811 Wayne County courthouse stood in the town of Salisbury, was moved to Richmond, then to the Fairgrounds at Centerville. Currentlly, it is being rebuilt near the Mansion House at Centerville. The original builder was Centerville resident William Commons. The second courthouse, built of brick, was also raised at Salisbury. The town of Salisbury has disappeared completely.

The first courthouse built in Richmond was designed by George Hoover (c. 1824-1879) in the Italianate style and faced South 4th Street. The county seat was moved from Centerville to Richmond in 1873 after lengthy dispute and vigorous opposition from residents of Centerville. As the photograph shows, the 1893 courthouse was completed before the older one was removed.

The third Wayne County courthouse stood at the northeast corner of Main and Morton streets in Centerville. This Greek Revival edifice later became Dunbar's hardware and furniture store, then their grocery.

In this scenario the railroads next came into play. In the 1850s and '60s Richmond gained several lines that provided north-south and east-west traffic. Richmond natives lobbied to obtain county seat status, and after fighting for possession of the county records, won the prize in 1873.

George Hoover, architect from Pennsylvania and Civil War veteran, designed an Italianate-style structure for the southwest corner of South 4th and Main streets. This proved satisfactory for nearly 20 years, but eventually more space was needed. The county commissioners hired James McLaughlin of Cincinnati as architect, approving his Richardsonian Romanesque style as expressing a "laudable solidarity and stability."

The present courthouse, in Richardsonian Romanesque style, was designed by James McLaughlin of Cincinnati, assisted by William Kaufman, Richmond architect/contractor.

The 1893 courthouse elevator proved quite durable before it was replaced by the present one.

The first women to serve on a jury in Wayne County outnumbered the men at a trial in 1923.

Richmond Law Enforcement

Designed in the late Italianate style, the Wayne County jail and sheriff's residence took up headquarters on South 2nd Street, near the present county Welfare Department.

In 1945 the Grand Jury inspected the Wayne County jail facility on South 2nd Street.

The new Wayne County Safety Building, containing the jail, was built on South 3rd Street, directly east of the former sheriff's house and jail, visible in the background.

A tender early photo of Nathaniel Bates with his daughters before committing his "crime of passion." After the axing, the girls went to live with his wife's mother. The axe handle is on display at the Wayne County Historical Museum.

The old jail yard is shown during the execution of Nathaniel Bates of Hagerstown, the last hanging in Wayne County, August 26, 1886. Bates was convicted of killing his wife at their home.

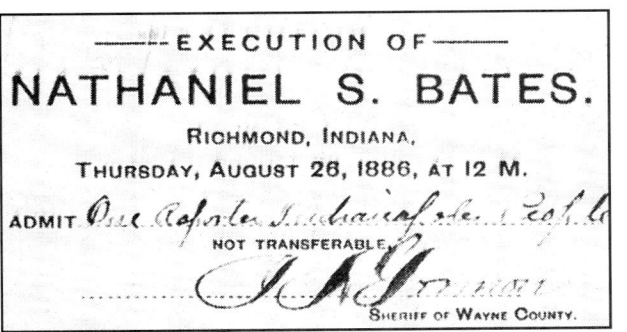

Tickets to the Bates hanging were issued to the press and notables of Wayne County by Sheriff Isaac Gormon.

In front of the police station on North 5th Street officials destroy barrels of illicit mash, probably during the Prohibition era.

131

Police Chiefs

In Richmond's early years, the head of the citizen-protection department was not called a police chief. Police leaders were called constables, marshals and superintendents.

Mayor Thomas W. Bennett (1831-1893), wearing his favorite slouch hat, stands in the back row of the police force. Bennett, a Civil War general, was Richmond's fifth mayor.

1834 Isaac Barnes first high constable	1886-1887 Joseph P. Iliff	1935-? Henry J. Vogelsong
1840 Jesse Meek, marshal	1890-1892 Albert G. Ogborn, marshal	1939-1948 Ellis H. Duckett
1857-1873 William Zimmerman marshal	1890-1891 John L. Bennett,	1948-1955 Lucas Rohe
1866 John S. Lyle,	1891-1892 Peter Kuhlman,	1956-1960 Dan Mitrione
1872-1873 Edward J. Salter	1893-1896 Henry G. Eggemeyer	1960-1966 Orville Conyers
1874-1882 L. O. Shofer, marshal	1897-1902 Charles W. Page	1966-1968 William Stultz
1874-1880 Alexander Horney	1903-1906 Isaac A. Gormon	1968-1973 Donald L. Strahan
1880-1882 Joseph D. Fleming	1907-1908 Jesse A. Bailey	1973-1974 Lewis E. Doren
1883-1889 John Fred Haner, marshal	1910-? Isaac A. Gormon	1974-1976 Louis E. Gibbs
1883-1884 Daniel Parshall,	1914-? Harry Goodwin	1976-1984 Charles R. Chris
1885-1886 J. J. Finney,	1918-? Isaac A. Gormon	1984-1990 Joseph A. Nimitz
	1921-1922 Roy M. Wenger	1989 Donald Ponder, acting chief
	1923-1930 William F. Eversman	1990 to present, Dennis R. Rice, Sr.
	1931-? Herbert Ray	

The police force of 1940 gathers on the steps of St. Mary's Catholic church for its group portrait.

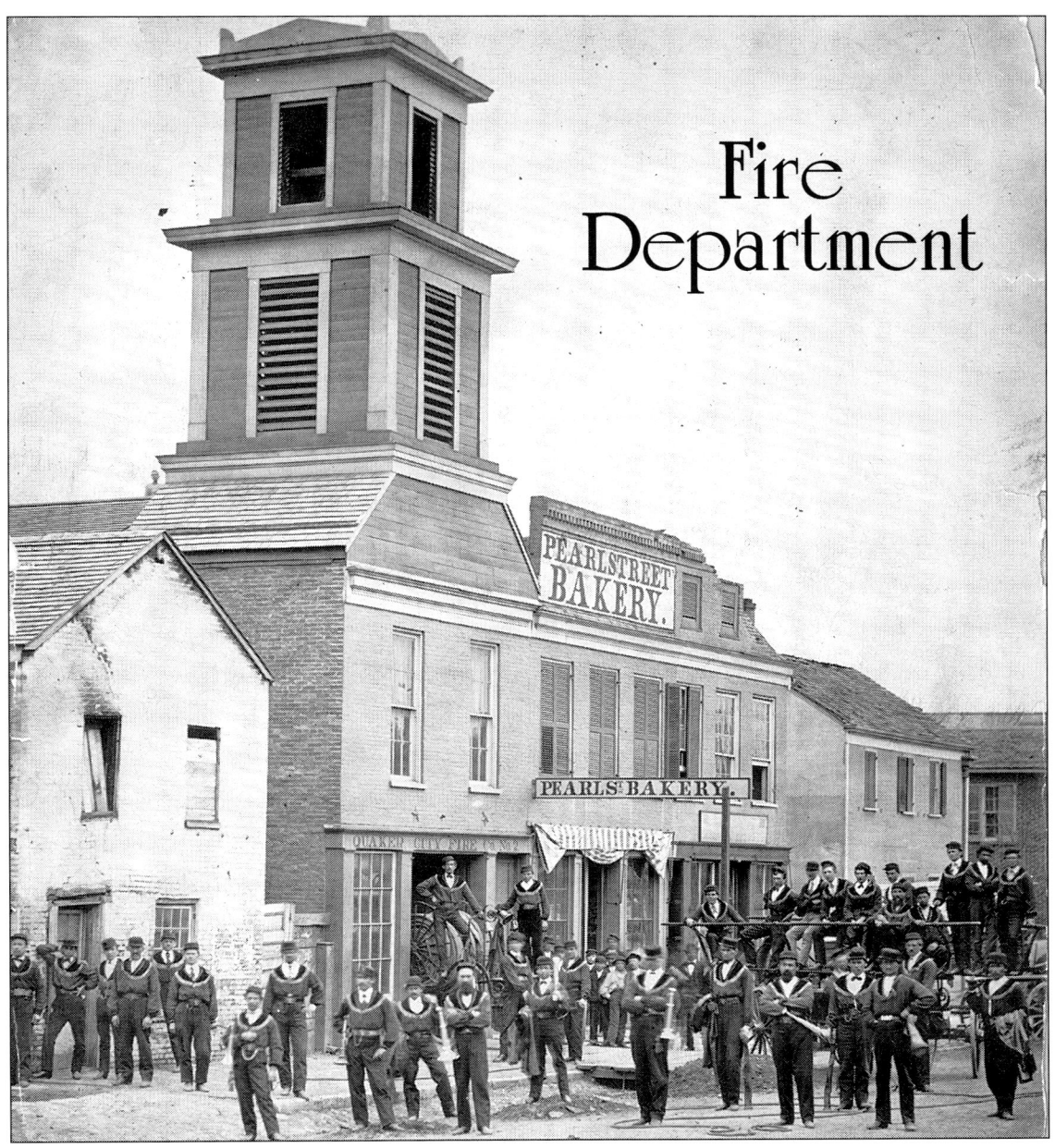

Fire Department

On December 6, 1830, 15 Richmond citizens met at A. Jefferis tavern on Fifth and Pearl to "protect themselves against the ravages of fire." In 1829 the fledgling community had already purchased a fire engine for $600, half of which was paid by corporate authorities and the other half by voluntary contributions of citizens.

An 1832 ordinance compelled Richmond citizens to choose 25 "stout" men to extinguish fires and to form an engine company which enjoyed plenary powers in conscripting citizens as a bucket brigade. In addition 20 other able-bodied men were chosen to form a Hook and Ladder Company. Lastly 15 citizens were to be named to form a Protection company "for the purpose of taking care of property in the time of fire."

This noble effort, however, terminated on January 6, 1834 when a new ordinance was adopted. Herein, the Engine company resigned their charge as there had been only occasional need for their services. The fire department's treasury totaling $1.50 was then turned over to the town authorities and Old Grindstone, the pioneer fire engine, was put out to pasture.

Until 1836 there was no interest in a fire department until a gentlemen from Boston sung the praises of a Yankee engine.

"Old Hunker," bought and christened in 1836, became Richmond's second fire engine. It was put on board in Boston harbor, transferred to a Mississippi steamboat arriving in Cincinnati in the dead of winter and loaded onto a prairie schooner.

This beauty with brakes gave working room for 24 men and wonder of wonders relieved the bucket company of their labors. A supply of water came from some large wells sunk in town.

The town slept more peacefully at night knowing that Old Hunker and the newly-formed more efficient company was on duty to protect them.

Richmond's first water pumper, the "Grindstone," was purchased in 1829. The hose was 10 feet long with a two-inch diameter nozzle. It took six men on a side to crank the water furnished to the box by buckets. Any citizen that did not "form themselves to be part of the Bucket Company," without excuse, was fined 50 cents as a corporate (town) fine.

This photo of volunteer firemen in their "fancy dress" uniforms was found in an attic of Station No. 4 at South 9th and E streets. An 1832 ordinance establishing a fire company stated that it was "the duty of the citizens to choose a company of stout, able-bodied men, 25 in number who had full power to impose fines compelling citizens to duty."

This steam fire engine was purchased in 1871 for the fire station located near Fort Wayne Avenue.

The Hope hose carrier with its bells and lanterns was bought in 1850 for Station No. 2.

The old No. 3 fire station was located where the later City building of 1890 was built.

Fire Chiefs

Richmond's believed-to-be first city directory in 1857 does not list a fire department; however, directories from 1859 till 1868 list companies called Old Hunker, Quaker City, Hoosier, Washington and Mechanics Steam. The 1868 directory is the first to list a fire department head, a chief engineer. It was not until the early 1900s that the title fire chief replaced chief engineer.

1868	Henry Downing
1870	J. F. Meyer
1872	I. G. Dougan
1881-1884	W. W. Alexander
1885-1886	William L Thomas
1887-1906	James Parsons
1907-1930	E. E. Miller
1931-1946	Harry Williams
1946-1959	Leslie Williams
1959-1964	Fred Klotz
1964-1966	Ernest Fredericks
1966-1968	Malvern Price
1968-1969	Donovan Johnson
1969-1975	William Berry
1975	John Newland
1976-1983	Paul (Moon) Mullin
1984-1985	Larry H. Bosell
1985	W. Joseph Pierce, acting administrator
1985-1986	David Harbin
1986-1989	Donald Trotter
1989 to present:	James A. Sticco

William Hanning and Joe Bates, standing, proudly display their fire equipment at the fire station at the intersection of South 9th and E streets.

Amos Bell, a relief driver, holds two of the handsome fire horses in front of Station No. 2, about 1915. Old Joe is at left and Dick, later renamed Bob, at right. The well-cared-for horses spent their retirement on the farm of W. E. Berry on Chester Pike.

Fire Chief Miller poses in his horse-drawn cart in front of the fire station in the old City building on North 5th Street.

The Fire Department was motorized by 1915, and Chief Miller shows off his sporty convertible.

Firemen are not always fighting fires. In this photo several of them are sharing a laugh with city officials at the station on North 8th Street. The facility was designed by John Hasecoster. The latter is mentioned often in Richmond history because he designed so many outstanding buildings. Hasecoster arrived in Richmond in 1867 from Germany. He continued his study in architecture in St. Louis and Chicago before returning to Richmond where his two brothers, Fred and George, owned a sash and door business.

The extensive J. C. Penney fire of 1942, at 719-21 Main Street, also involved the Loehr-Klute clothing store.

Three youngsters join the crowd viewing the J. C. Penney fire of 1942. Imitating their fathers who were fighting in World War II, the boys are wearing their small scale uniforms.

The day after the J. C. Penney fire a large crowd of spectators gathered to look at the wreckage.

On January 2, 1944, a fire demolished the Coliseum that stood on the east side of North 7th Street between Main and North A streets. The city lost an important auditorium and sports arena. It occupied the site of a former cigar box factory.

Fire Stations

The old South Side or "Wooden shoes" fire station on the southwest corner of South E and Garden streets was manned primarily by men of German heritage who often wore their wooden clogs. The structure was razed in 1927.

Pictured is the Central Fire Station located in the 1886 City building on North 5th Street. The photo was taken after the department was motorized and the horses put out to pasture.

No. 3 Fire station at 1515 North A street has been remodeled and is now known as Autohaus. A major reason for having a tower was to hang the wet hoses for adequate drying. The top of the tower was removed.

Station No. 4, located at South 9th and E streets, is another of John Hasecoster's designs. The top of this tower also has been removed. The white monument near the entrance lists the regiments that mustered in at Richmond's Camp Wayne during the Civil War.

Station No. 5 on North West 5th Street was originally in a Spanish or Mediterranean style and later remodeled into apartments.

City Buildings...

The first recorded location in Richmond where city business was conducted was on September 14, 1818, at the house of Thomas & Justice. The latter were carpenters who built a new frame structure at the northeast corner of Main and Front streets. It was designed as a store. The village trustees who attended included Ezra Boswell, the brewer "with his mutilated eye;" John McLane, the blacksmith "with his ample physical frame" and Thomas Swain, president of the meeting "a dark-skinned, stoop-shouldered man of solid sense." Such was the beginning of Richmond.

Dr. Ithamar Warner (1782-1835) left his estate, including his office on the east side of North 5th Street, to the city. The facility was then used as the City Building and mayor's office. At left the Fire station, then called No. 3, is visible. These buildings were used until 1886 when new ones were erected from a John Hasecoster design.

Removal of its decorative tower and finials significantly changed the character of the City Building of 1886.

And the place where business was conducted. The first business at hand was what to name the city. Smithville was suggested, named after the proprietor, John Smith who erected a large brick home in 1811 at what became Market Street, west of Front. The Indians including famed warrior, Tecumseh, came to trade there. The other lot-holders present voted in the name Richmond.

Since the time of that first historical meeting in a carpenter's house, Richmond government has been conducted in sundry facilities and locations over a span of 175 years.

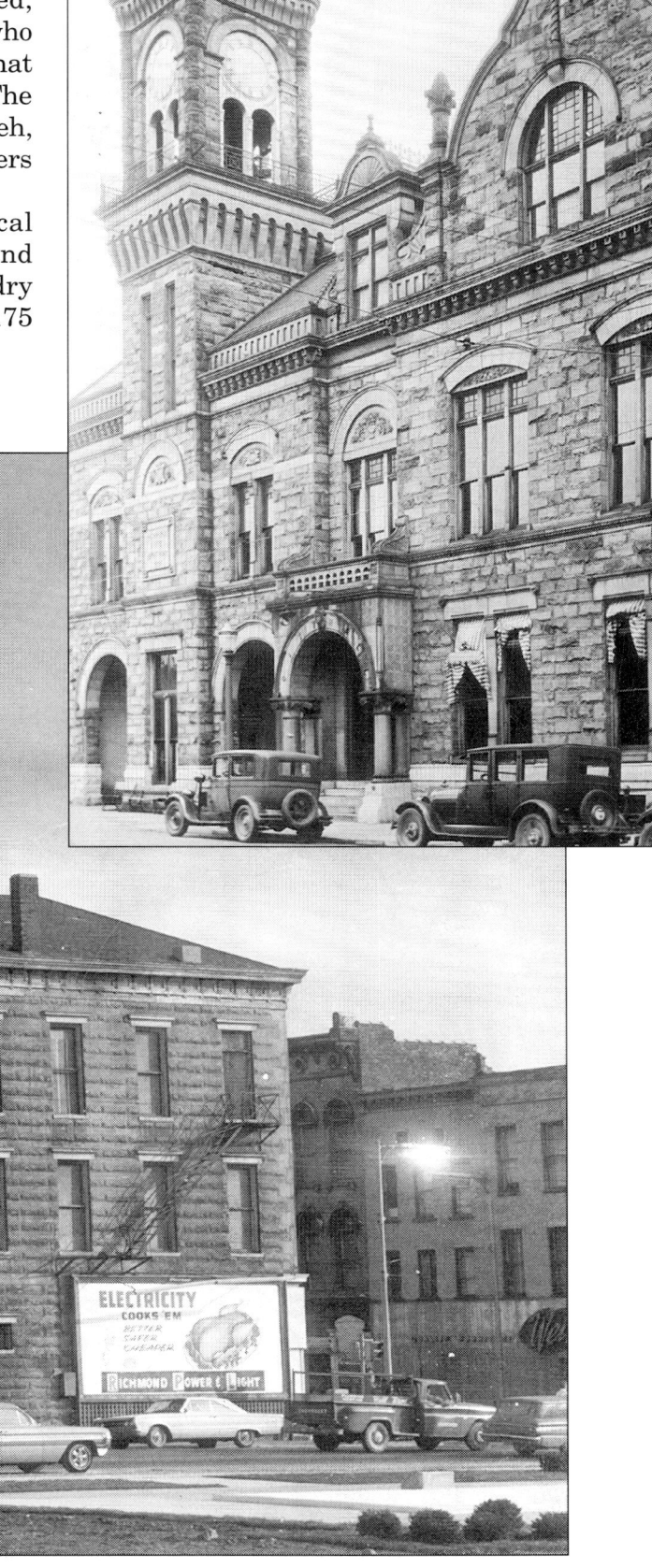

The castle-like City Building of 1886 is shown basking in the glory of its elaborate Romanesque style.

First mayor, John Sailor (1781-c. 1871), was born in Philadelphia and came to Richmond in 1831. A borough charter was issued to Richmond in 1834 and Sailor was chosen as first burgess, presiding officer of the city council. Richmond was incorporated as a city in 1840 and Sailor was elected mayor. By trade he was a cabinet- and carriage-maker. In 1852 he was succeeded as mayor by John Finley. Two years later Sailor and his wife moved to Griggsville, Illinois. In 1871 at the age of 90 years, he climbed a ladder to pick cherries. He was found on the ground, unconscious and badly bruised. His death day is uncertain.

John Finley (1797-1866), second mayor of Richmond, was born in Virginia and came to this area in 1821. Trained in the tannery business, he first managed that enterprise for John Smith, one of the city founders. After one season he became a justice of the peace, was elected to the Indiana House and then to the Senate, became part owner of the *Palladium* in 1834, and served as clerk of the Wayne County court in 1837. A poem he wrote in 1833, "The Hoosier's Nest," was published in an Indianapolis newspaper and popularized the term "Hoosier," meaning a sturdy, hard-working pioneer. Finley was elected mayor in 1852 and was kept in office until his death in 1866.

Dr. William W. Zimmerman (1855-1922) was a cabinetmaker for 14 years before earning his medical degree. He was a three-time mayor: 1898-1905, 1910-1913, and 1918-1922.

Frank Waltermann, 27th mayor of Richmond, was in office from 1984-1991. He is the son of Joseph M. Waltermann, mayor from 1935-1938.

Richmond's newest City complex features multiple columns. It is said that the contractor installed them upside down. Many structures designed by Frank Lloyd Wright show similar columns-resembling golf tees supporting the roof.

Mayor Joseph M. Waltermann (1884-1960) turned the mechanism directing city sewage into a treatment area on June 30, 1936. Advanced waste treatment plants reduced pollution of the Whitewater River.

The Richmond Water Works plant was built before 1896, remodeled in 1912 and located south of the New Paris Pike.

Ulysses Parks was employed by the Home Telephone Company to drive to fires and ensure protection of the telephone lines.

When these telephone operators were on duty in 1896, there was a human voice serving the customers asking their numbers. The site pictured is believed to be at 832 Main Street.

James M. Starr (1824-1900), son of Charles and Elizabeth Starr, early settlers of Richmond, was involved in many business and civic ventures, including the Richmond Gas Company. Natural gas was obtained from the well-known "gas belt" near Anderson, Muncie, and Winchester that supplied many glass factories in those cities.

When natural gas was discovered in Indiana the populace did not realize that it could be depleted. The wells were often burned day and night and before long the gas was gone. Richmond was less affected than some cities and turned to the manufacture of fuel by the water-gas process. This was done by burning a mixture of coal and coke in a generator, dousing it with water, then forcing the gas into storage tanks. Later, gas was brought in from other locations. The large storage tank at the east end of the Main Street Bridge would be filled during the night and gradually collapse during the day.

Below: The Richmond Gas Company building, in Italianate style, is located just east of where the storage tank stood, on the north side of Main Street. It is listed on the National Register of Historic Places.

Orange V. Lemon, Jr., and his family had a great sense of humor so when natural gas was being depleted they posed for the photographer around the wood or coal stove in their parlor at 22 North 17th Street. Mr. Lemon was proud of his heritage as an "Orangeman," a Protestant from Ireland.

1968 Explosion

Firemen attempted to control the blaze that erupted after explosions at Marting Arms Company and Vigran's Variety Store at the intersection of South 6th and Main streets on April 6, 1968. A total of 41 people died and many more were injured as more than a city block was leveled. Many shoppers were in stores because it was a warm day and the last Saturday before Easter. *Ralph Pyle photo.*

No clear blame has been placed for the explosion and fire, but it is possible that leaking gas might have contributed to the fires that broke out in the downtown area. Part of the clean-up was hampered because gun cartridges in the Marting Arms basement continued to explode. The Elder-Beerman store has been built along the Promenade in the general vicinity of the blast. *Ralph Pyle photo.*

The Wayne County Office of Civil Defense quickly put its staff into action and coordinated the volunteer effort. Only essential workers were allowed in the area of damage although sightseers came from miles around. A memorial monument to those who died has been placed west of the intersection of 6th Street and the Promenade. The remarkable photographs were taken by Ralph Pyle whose photo studio was nearby and who had seen wartime action in Korea.

Heavy bricks have been piled along the sidewalk for the first paving of Richmond's Main Street.

Richmond's first sewer was one of the largest built in the city. It was six feet in diameter, made of stone, and extended from 8th Street through Washington Avenue and Gaar, Scott & Company, to its exit into the Whitewater River.

The Municipal Light Plant on Johnson Street near the east bank of the Whitewater River was considered state-of-the-art for its day; built in 1901.

The photo shows the interior of the former U. S. Post Office at the southwest corner of 9th and North A streets.

Some Richmond natives believe that the former U. S. Post Office, built of Indiana oolitic limestone in the Beaux Art style, is far superior in architectural design to the present one.

Thanks to the foresight of Don McBride, the edifice currently houses the Indiana Football Hall of Fame Museum.

Richmond Bridges

For a community on the edge of a gorge about 80 feet deep bridges are a necessity. Before there was a bridge at the west end of Main Street people, horses and wagons traveled down the sloping riverbank and forded the shallows in the vicinity of South E Street.

This caused the east side of Richmond to grow more rapidly than the west side. Not all traffic was from the east, however, because many settlers came from the southern part of the state on trails paralleling some of the 127 miles of streams. Many covered bridges were built to cross such streams.

Once the railroads started coming through in the 1850s it was essential to have stable bridges for them to cross the streams and especially the Whitewater Gorge. The first railroad bridge spanned the Gorge in 1853 and in 1885 the Doran bridge connected North D Street with Richmond Avenue. To provide another route to the west side of the city, the South G Street bridge was opened in 1932.

A workman carrying his lunch pail crosses the swinging bridge over the West Fork of the Whitewater River in Happy Hollow. Mount Auburn, now called Newman's Hill, is visible in the background. It was once the site of a recreation park.

The bridge for the Pennsylvania Railroad over the Whitewater River was built in 1902.

A postcard view shows the Main Street bridge built in 1921 over the Whitewater River. Facing northeast, one can see the large storage tank of the Richmond Gas Company.

An old covered bridge on National Road West crossed Clear Creek near Earlham Cemetery.

Members of the South Side Improvement Association helped to turn the first soil for the building of the South G Street bridge. Adolph W. Blickwedel, a cabinetmaker, railroader, and later grocer, was president of the association that had encouraged the building of a bridge at that location for 15 years.

The South G Street bridge is an important link between the main part of the city and the west side, near Richmond Senior High School. The bridge was dedicated and officially opened July 10, 1932, with Wilfred Jessup as master of ceremonies and Judge G. H. Hoelscher as speaker. The cost was $220,000 and I. E. Smith, Richmond contractor, was the successful bidder.

Richmond Public Library

Richmond people always have appreciated books, and the first permanent library was built in 1864 from funds donated by noted businessman, Robert Morrisson. The Dugdale family sold their land at the southwest corner of North 6th and A streets for the project. The architect was Allen W. Cornell. A residence for the librarian was provided at the rear of the building with its entrance on North A street.

The Morrisson-Reeves Library of 1893 was designed by John Hasecoster in the Romanesque style. Funds donated by Caroline Middleton Reeves provided for expansion and a new design for the library.

Robert Morrisson (1786-1865) who came to Indiana from North Carolina in 1810, was successful in all of his business ventures and made notable charitable and benevolent donations. His portrait hangs in the Morrisson-Reeves Library. He was a brother-in-law of Jeremiah Cox, Sr., one of Richmond's founders.

Mrs. Sarah Finley Wrigley (1830-c. 1919), daughter of Mayor John Finley, was married to Benjamin Wrigley who died at the close of the Civil War. She was the city's second librarian, following Jesse Brown who left at the end of two months to be superintendent of a school system in Wayne County. Wrigley served as librarian from 1864 to 1903. She died at the home of her son, Luke, a lawyer and judge at Albion, Indiana.

Ada Stubbs Bernhardt (1858-1946), third Richmond librarian, was in that position 42 years. She was a daughter of Mayor Lewis Stubbs and a sister of Edna S. Cathell, the artist. Bernhardt received the A. B. degree from Earlham College in 1879, and also attended the University of Illinois.

The interior of the Morrisson-Reeves Library contained an attractive spiral stairway that was moved to the present library.

The 1975 Morrisson-Reeves Library was designed by Jack Hodell of Cincinnati and built during the administration of Harriet Bard. The present librarian is Carol Smyth.

People Serving People

In early Richmond the infirm relied on relatives, friends or servants to care for them during an illness. That was until a new facility, St. Stephen's Hospital, opened in 1884. A residence at 301 North 8th Street was converted into a ten-bed hospital by the Women's Auxiliary of St. Paul's Episcopal Church. The building currently exists as an apartment house.

General Rules of St. Stephen's Hospital.

Reid Memorial Hospital, built in 1905, was sited near the home of Col. John Miller on Chester Boulevard. The Miller house was used as the nurses' residence for many years. Most of the funding came from Daniel G. Reid, the architect was John Hasecoster and the style is Romanesque. (Hasecoster continued to be popular because he showed an acceptance and understanding of new styles as they came into vogue.)

The Social Service Bureau of the American Red Cross provided a home nursing service to the community, using a fleet of Ford cars for transport. Many women had learned to drive by the mid-1920s.

Nurses and staff of the Social Service Bureau were photographed at their headquarters on 111 North 8th Street. Esther Barker Neff, at right, was associated with the Red Cross for many years.

The Salvation Army on North 12th Street used a building that later became Townsend Community Center. The Salvation Army currently takes up residence at 100 South 4th Street.

A reunion of the 84th Infantry Regiment was held September 20, 1883 at Dublin, Indiana. the men had been mustered in at Richmond on September 8, 1862 under Col. Nelson Trusler and their first military duty was the defense of Covington, Kentucky, and Cincinnati. The regiment was retired from service on June 14, 1865 at Nashville, Tennessee.

Company F of the 161st Indiana Infantry formed in Richmond in 1898 to serve in the Spanish-American War. After medical examinations, they camped at Glen Miller Park, renamed for the occasion as Camp Ostrander after the mayor. They were then ordered to Jacksonville, Florida, where they waited again before proceeding to Havana as part of the Army of Occupation. They returned to Richmond on May 3, 1899. Paul Comstock was first lieutenant.

Company K of the Indiana State Militia was sent to Lake County in 1919 to help keep order during a steel workers' strike. They spent 17 days at Indiana Harbor and East Chicago. The company formed in Richmond in 1917.

A crowd of 3,000 attended the ceremony at Conservation Park June 9, 1946, dedicating a memorial plaque bearing the names of Richmond and Wayne Township men killed on the battlefields of World War II. Principal speaker was Marine Brig. Gen. Christian F. Schilt and flowers were strewn from a plane piloted by James Lemon, a former Navy dive bomber pilot.

Chapter 6: Family Life in Richmond

The second grade of Finley School in 1912, located at South B Street between 4th and 5th streets. Note the Roman numerals on the blackboard on the right as well as the emphasis placed on fine penmanship.

Churches-Schools-Sports-Homes

Churches

Their aversion to the enslavement of other humans motivated the early Quakers who came to the Northwest Territory and to Indiana. Their religious meetings were held initially in residences. When a group was large enough, a request would be sent to an established meeting to form a new monthly meeting. When permission was granted, a simple meetinghouse would be built, always without a spire.

Methodists are considered the next group to have come to this area, often under the care of a circuit-riding minister. Baptists met at a Gaar home south of Richmond.

Scotch-Irish Presbyterians, German Lutherans and Catholics, Irish Catholics, Episcopalians, all came in large numbers as the city grew. Today the churches of Richmond fill more than two pages of telephone book listings.

Shown above is the Indiana Yearly Meetinghouse on North F Street, begun in 1823 and finished in 1829. Another view taken from a Mote stereoptican slide is shown below.

St. John's Lutheran Church and parsonage, about 1875. The second floor and tower had been added to the original 1843 church. The pastor often used the adjacent two-story building to the right of the church, at 322 South 4th Street, as a parsonage. The home now houses attractive apartments.

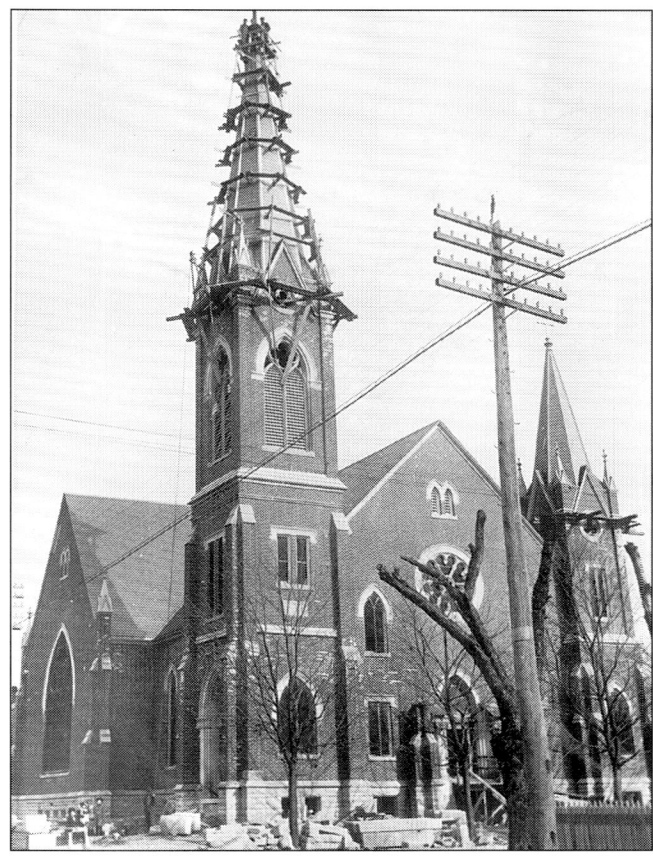

The St. John's Lutheran Church congregation moved to their new church with a festive procession in 1902. The architect was John Hasecoster.

One of the finest examples of Greek Revival architecture in the city was the Methodist Episcopal Church at North 5th and A streets. The church was torn down to make away for the entrance to the U.S. Post Office.

The First Presbyterian Church initially met at 115 South 4th Street until their facility on South 8th Street was completed in 1854. The steeple was struck by lightning on August 22, 1885 and the resulting fire did considerable damage. A new building was raised at 100 North 10th Street and dedicated in 1887. The older structure was purchased by the Knights of Pythias who remodeled it for their lodge.

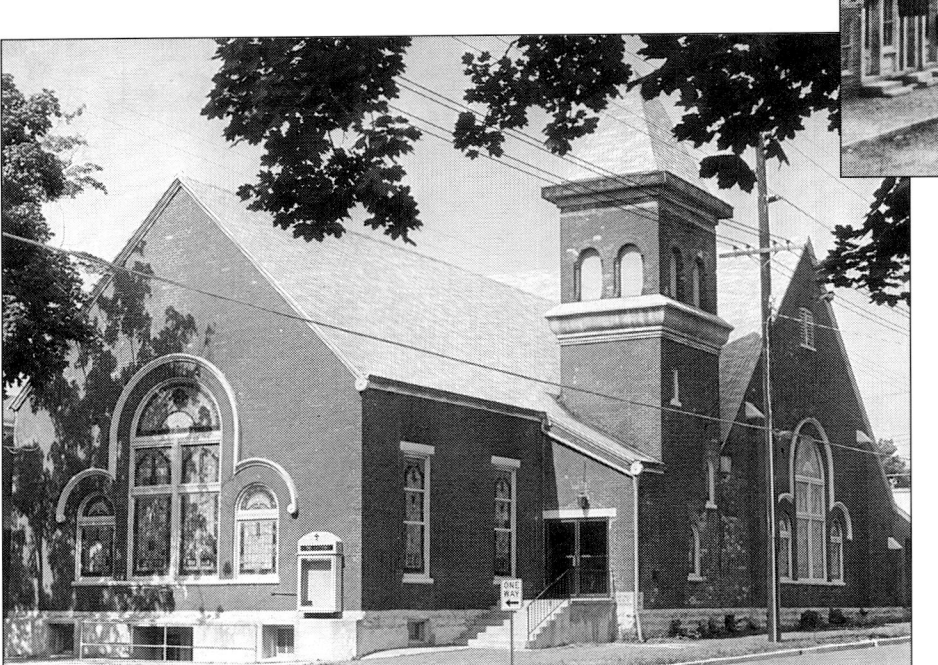

Bethel African Methodist Episcopal Church was organized in 1838 by Rev. William Paul Quinn, a native of northern India. Fifteen members met at the home of Cornelius Overman, 419 South 5th Street, and then purchased a frame building at 425 South 6th Street. The present church at 200 South 6th Street was bought in 1868, and a new church home was put up in 1893.

The congregation of Central Methodist Church used this columned Greek Revival style on the southwest corner of North 10th and A streets until their new building at 1425 East Main Street was consecrated in 1958. The earlier edifice was then torn down.

160

This United Brethren Church at 200 North 11th Street was originally built to serve United Presbyterians, the parent congregation of Reid Memorial Presbyterian. The building is now called Olde North Chapel and is used for weddings and meetings.

The laying of the cornerstone and the dedication of Reid Memorial Church took place in 1904.

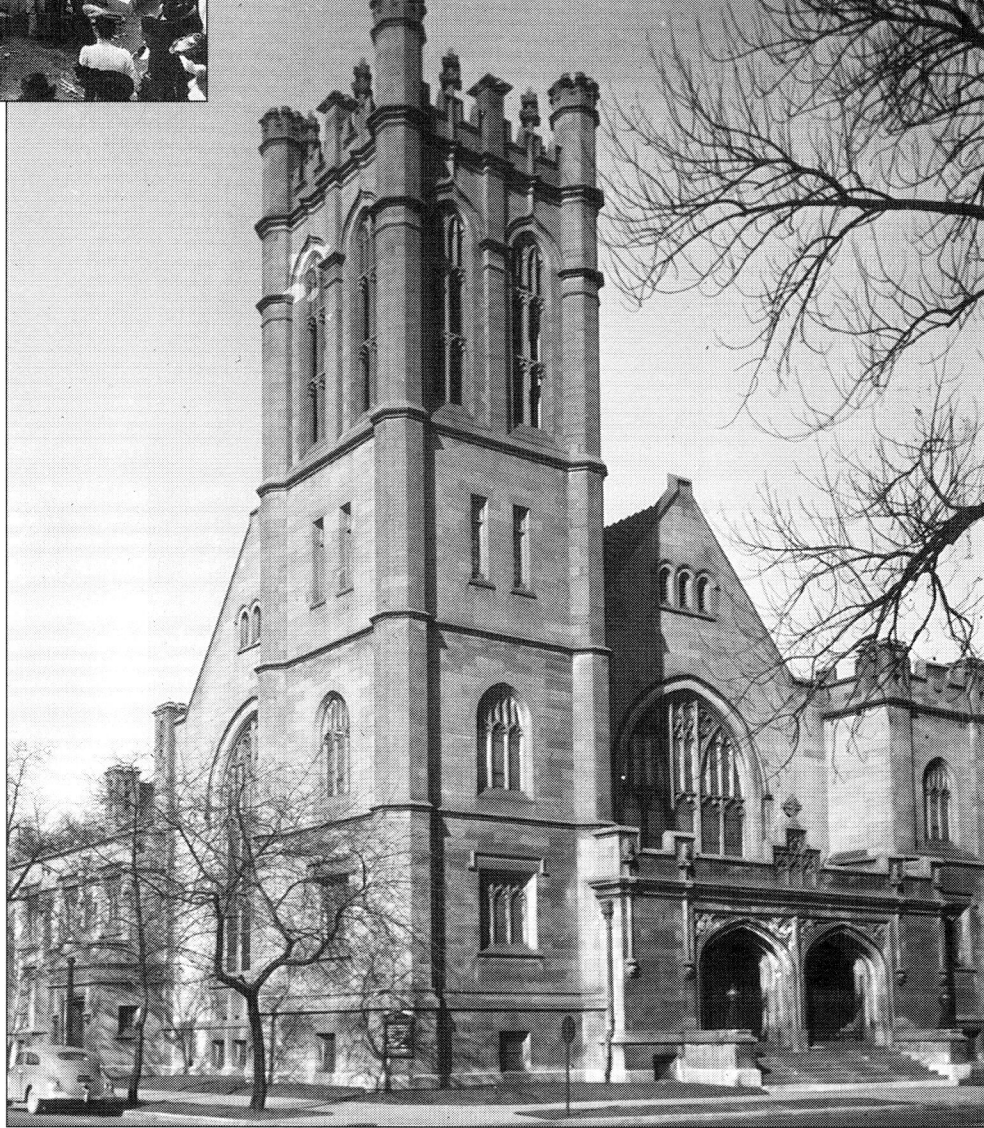

Reid Memorial Presbyterian Church at 1004 North A Street, funded mainly by Daniel G. Reid, boasts several beautiful Tiffany windows. The Scottish Gothic structure is made from Indiana limestone.

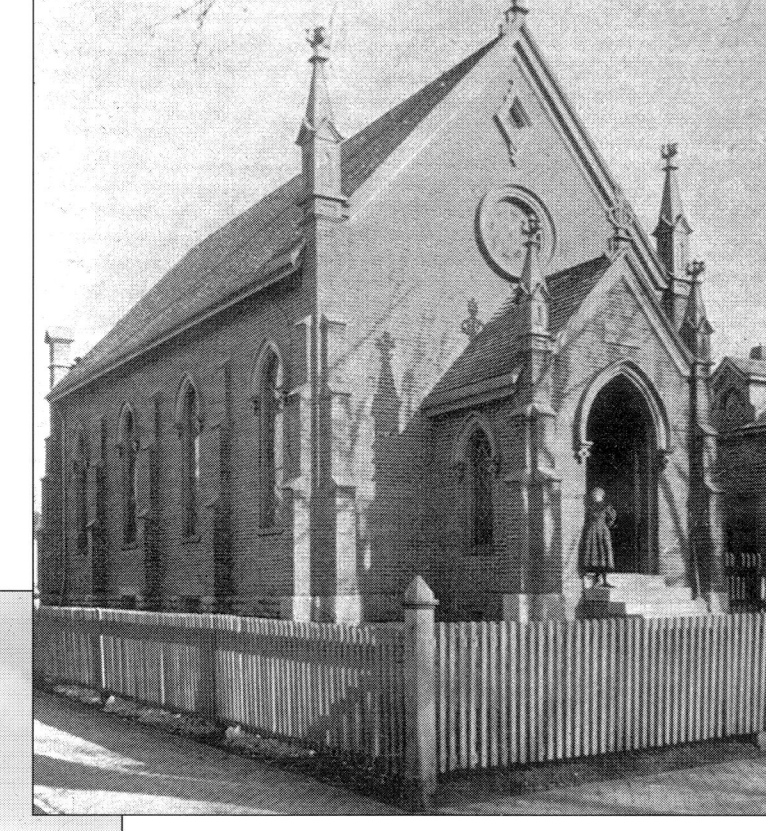

The New Jerusalem or Swedenborgian Church was built at the southeast corner of South 7th and A streets in the Ecclesiastical Gothic style. The pastor, Rev. George Field, an Oxford graduate, arrived from England in May of 1870.

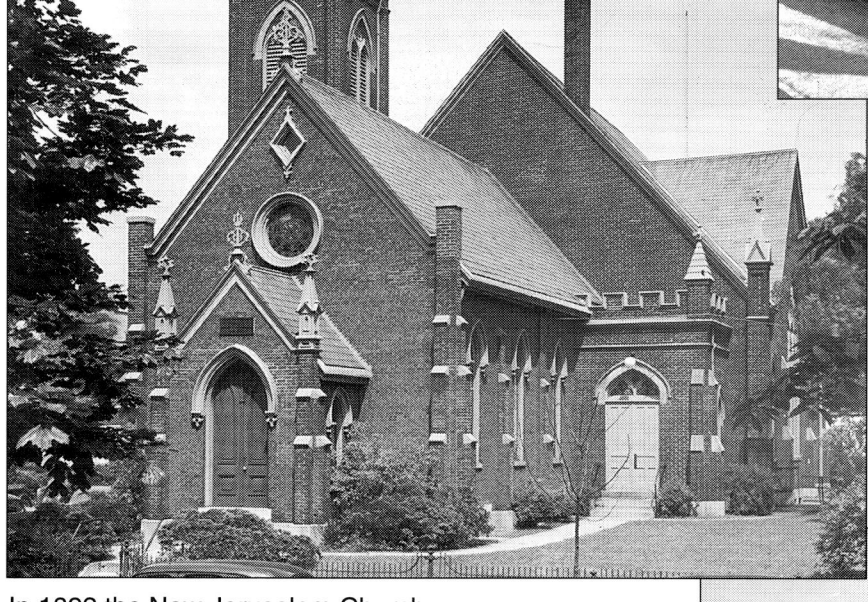

In 1892 the New Jerusalem Church was remodeled and enlarged to become home to the Trinity English Lutheran congregation.

The First Baptist Church at 16 North 11th Street was organized in 1865 with 22 members by Rev. J. B. Angebroad. The early services were held in Engine House No. 3 on North 5th Street and later in Phillips Hall at 6th and Main streets. This building dates to 1871 and was replaced in 1957 with one at 1601 South A Street.

The Original Church of God at 811 North 14th Street celebrated its 50th anniversary in 1981.

Vallie Burrell is credited with founding the Original Church of God. She was aided by her cousin, Anna Mae Fanning.

Christ Tabernacle Church was founded in 1928 when Elder Grey and his wife, Gustavia Lewis Grey, came to Richmond from Fort Wayne. After several other pastors served the growing church Elder Adam Pope and his wife, shown in the front row, helped raise the church structure at 56 North West H Street. The congregation moved to a former Lutheran church at 248 Pearl Street in 1974 and were able to burn the mortgage in 1985.

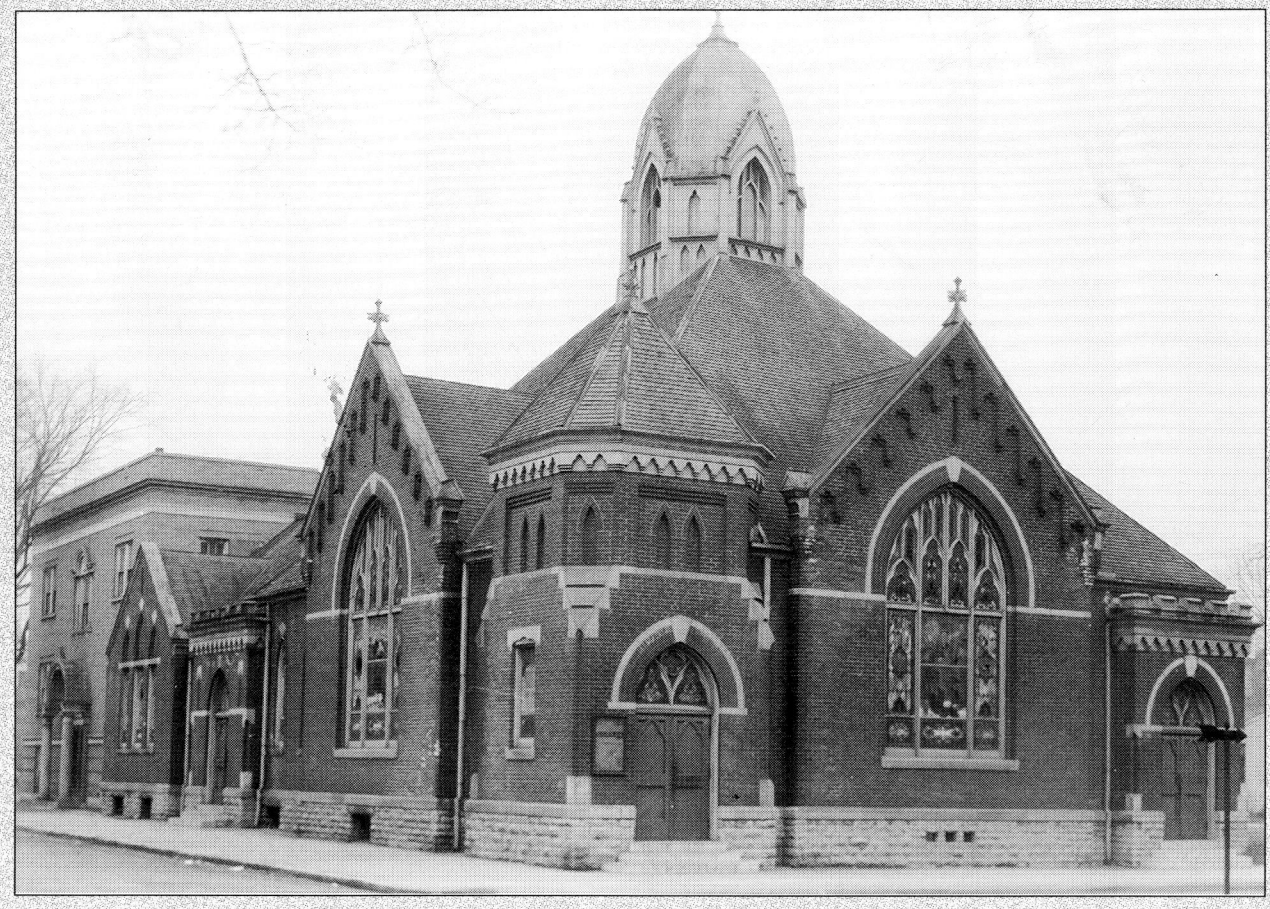

First Christian Church used the annex erected in 1917 for worship services while the sanctuary was torn down and the present building erected at the southwest corner of South 10th and A streets.

First English Lutheran Church was built in 1885 at the southwest corner of South 11th and A streets. German was spoken in the early Lutheran churches, and the designation "English" meant that the congregation had opted to use the language of their adopted country.

St. Paul's Episcopal Church built in 1854 served a congregation established in 1838. The church often appears in watercolor drawings by Lefevre J. Cranstone, an Englist artist who visited relatives in Richmond in 1859-60. The tower has been modified.

St. Mary's Catholic Church, 710 North A Street, has its rectory on the site of the Dr. James Hibberd house. Hibberd (1816-1903) was Richmond's eighth mayor and was also elected to two terms as president of the American Medical Society. To the left is the site of the original St. Mary's. The parsonage was dedicated in 1908, the church in 1913, and the school, at far left, in 1939.

Earlham College

The impressive entranceway of Earlham College extends south from National Road West. The college was founded in 1847 as a boarding school through the efforts of many local Quakers. Most of the land was purchased from the Jesse Bond family.

Earlham College started as a Friend's Boarding School in 1847, following a pattern in Quaker education found to be successful in England and on the East Coast. Initially there was only one building that housed classrooms, administrative offices, dining hall and living quarters. A farmhouse that came with the purchase of the land held married teachers until it was removed in 1883.

Elijah Coffin, a native of North Carolina, a teacher, storekeeper and then a Richmond banker, was especially diligent in support of the school. In 1859 the assemblage at the Indiana Yearly Meeting agreed that the boarding school should become a college. It was named after Earlham Hall, in Norwich, England, home of the Gurney family of Quakers.

In 1856 a valuable telescope was purchased after the first of many fund-raising projects by the alumni. The observatory to house the telescope opened in 1861 and was distinguished as the first such structure on an Indiana campus. Natural science has been a strongly supported discipline at Earlham and the next building, Parry Hall, was designed to house chemistry and physics classes.

The college has attracted devoted teachers and students who have ranked high in their preparatory work. Many have gone on to become teachers at all levels. In general, there is a strong service ethic among the graduates of Earlham College.

Lindley Hall, erected in 1887, contained administrative and faculty offices, classrooms and a natural history museum. Designed by architect Thomas Harrison, the building was destroyed by fire in the early morning of October 23, 1924. One fireman was killed when a wall toppled.

The first astronomical observatory in Indiana was constructed at Earlham in 1861.

Edwin Bundy Hall, a dormitory built in 1907, was designed by William Kaufman, Richmond architect and contractor. It was named for the son of Zenas and Rachel A. Bundy of Greenfield, a student from 1897 to 1899.

Left: The graduating class of 1882 as a class memorial donated this elaborate fountain on the east side of Earlham Hall. The center was topped with a figure of Cupid, often removed as a joke by other students. Eventually the center part was removed, but the base remained for many years and was the source of some invertebrate specimens for biology classes.

The cost of raising Parry Chemistry Hall was funded in 1887 by Mordecai Parry, local lumber dealer and carriage maker. The main floor contained a lecture room seating 100 and the physics laboratory. The chemistry lab was set up on the second floor. One of the college's distinguished professors of chemistry was Dr. Ernest A. Wildman. The hall was demolished in 1954 to provide space for another dormitory, Barrett Hall.

The Earlham Library of 1901 has become the Social Science Building. Initial funding was provided by the Board of Trustees, faculty, alumni and by library philanthropist, Andrew Carnegie.

The Earlham commencement of 1870 appears to have been held under the trees at Chase stage.

Carpenter Hall in 1927 replaced Lindley Hall and is named in honor of Walter (1811-1910) and Susanna Carpenter, early officials of Earlham College. Walter served as superintendent, trustee and committee member for a total of 35 years. He is credited with planting most of the campus trees, including more than 20 native forest species.

An Earlham May Day procession of 1969 shows the team of oxen hauling the traditional Maypole for the festivities. The ceremony is held at four-year intervals and involves the entire campus community.

Thomas E. Jones (1888-1973) received his degree from Earlham in 1912, attended Hartford Seminary and Columbia University, and taught courses in religion at Earlham in 1915-16. He studied and taught in Japan from 1917-24 before becoming president of Fisk University, a position he held for 20 years. He was chosen president of Earlham in 1946, retiring in 1958. Several buildings were added to the campus during these years, including Barrett Hall, Olvey-Andis Hall, Dennis Science Hall, Stout Memorial Meetinghouse, Teague Library and a new Earlham Hall. A soil research project was enlarged under the leadership of James Thorp, noted soil scientist.

Clara Comstock (c.1879-1966), daughter of Daniel Comstock, a prominent Richmond lawyer, city attorney and judge, began to teach physical education at Earlham in 1915 after attending the University of Chicago. She taught from 1915-1949, was dean of women from 1929-1946, and dean of personnel from 1946-1949. She directed several of the quadrennial May Day programs and in 1929 encouraged the purchase of two riding horses for the college.

A mastodon from the Bookout farm in Randolph County is housed in Joseph Moore Museum, an annex of the David Worth Dennis Science Hall, built in 1952. After the Lindley Hall fire the mastodon bones were stored until they were reassembled in the new museum by James Cope, museum director, along with a staff of assistants.

Joseph Moore (1832-1905) apparently carried his easel and blackboard with its drawing of a crayfish to the photographer's studio. Moore entered the Friends Boarding School, later renamed Earlham, in the spring of 1853 and became an assistant teacher that same fall. In 1859 he attended Harvard College, taking advanced courses for two years, before returning to Earlham in 1861. He was given a leave from 1865 to 1868 to help with reconstruction of Quaker schools in North Carolina, one of which later became Guilford College. Moore presided as president of Earlham from 1868 to 1883 and was geologist and museum curator from 1888 to 1905.

Belle Vue Place has gone by several names in its interesting past. Opening as Greenmount Seminary in 1851, the school closed in 1858 and was sold to Dr. James Gross who offered "water cures" at Greenmount Retreat. Renamed Belle Vue Place in 1869, Dr. Charles Pearson of Indianapolis advertised treatment for epilepsy, paralysis, chorea and all forms of nervous disease. This lasted until 1874 when Dr. E. Small took over specializing in the medical and surgical treatment of women.

Wernle Orphans' Home

The former Greenmount/Belle Vue property at 2000 Wernle Road was given a new educational life in 1879 when it became the home for orphaned or fatherless children under the direction of Richmond's St. John's Lutheran Church. Other Lutheran congregations assisted financially, and it was named for Rev. Carl Wernle, a pastor from Galion, Ohio.

When Wernle Orphans' Home opened it cared for children from Lutheran families. Eventually the home embraced children from other denominations and also expanded its treatment center. Carl Lash was superintendent from 1954-1965 with a staff of 15. Rev. Paul E. Knecht, present executive director, now heads a staff of 150. The group shown here was attending a reunion.

An early Wayne County school was established on the farm of Jonathan Roberts at the northeast corner of South 13th and A streets. The home was built in 1812 for Nathan and Rebecca Hawkins when they moved closer to Richmond for protection against Indian raids. The cabin is now found on the grounds of the Wayne County Historical Museum on North A Street.

Early Schools

The last one-room school in the Richmond area is on the Boston Pike south of the city, still standing, but in dilapidated condition.

The former St. Mary's Catholic School was located on the southeast corner of North A and 6th streets. It was replaced by the current Seton East School facility.

Garfield School stood at the northeast corner of South 12th and A streets.

Morton High School, now the Cigna Insurance Company at 120 North 9th Street. Nine colorful terra cotta plaques depicting occupations are over the arched windows on the east facade.

Richmond High School, 380 Hub Etchison Parkway, looks over the Whitewater Gorge.

Richmond High School

Obtaining a high school education was not an easy task in the early days of Richmond. Although the local population was generally literate, time was precious when farm and household tasks were onerous. People had to be fed and clothed first, then they could think about education.

The one-room log schools were scarce, teachers were often itinerant, and books were nonexistent. A piece of slate was valuable.

Richmond's Quakers are credited with organizing elementary schools as early as 1810. The first high school teacher was Issac Hiatt who taught in a brick schoolhouse in 1836. Barnabas C. Hobbs taught in the same school in 1843 and went on to teach at Friends Boarding School, eventually becoming the first president of Earlham College.

Hiram Hadley started his Normal Academy in 1856 and taught for seven years. He also helped organize teachers' institutes and the State Teachers' Association. Hadley later moved to the southwest where he became president of the University of New Mexico.

The first city high school is believed to have been started in 1864-65 under the guidance of Jesse H. Brown, the man who had been named first librarian for Morrisson Library. He was librarian for only two months, then was named superintendent of schools. Several sites were used for high school classes, including rooms in the parochial schools church basements and dwellings.

The more recent structures designed for high school classes have been Garfield School, Morton High School, now the Cigna building, and the present high school on Hub Etchison Parkway.

A workman stokes the furnace at Sevastopol School in the Fairview area of West Richmond.

The well-stocked library at Richmond High School is quiet and empty in this early photograph.

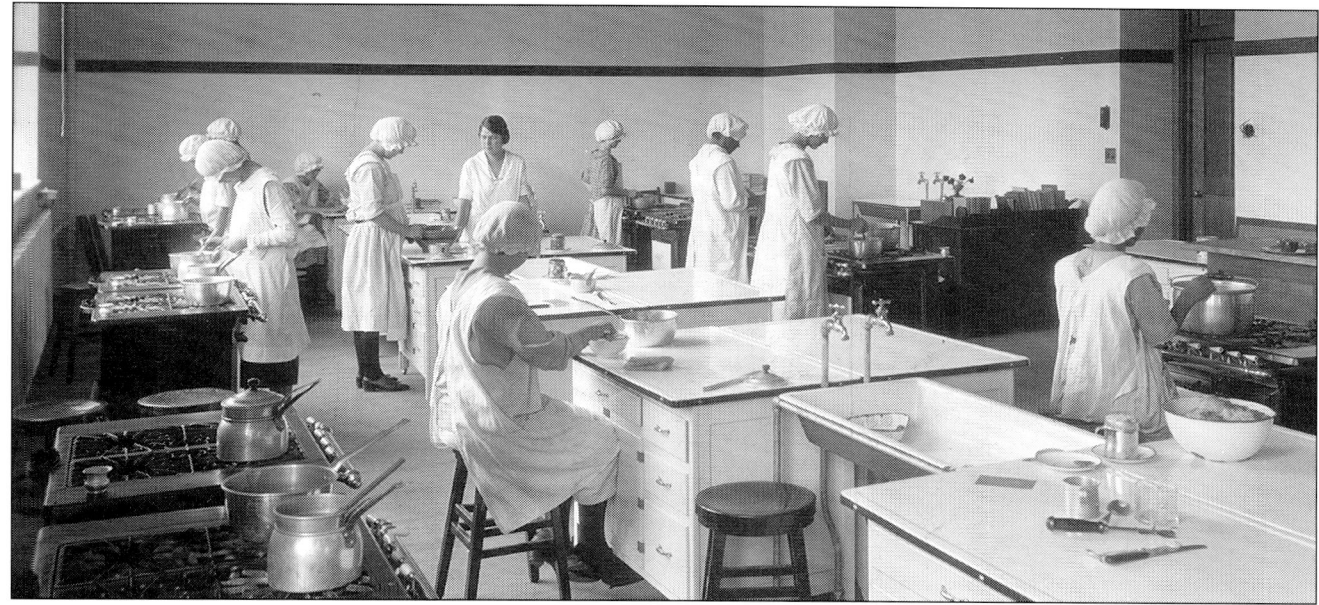

Home economics class prepares a meal, probably at Morton High School on North 9th Street. For sanitary reasons the girls wore protective head covering.

An early-day industrial arts class at Morton High School.

The Art Association of Richmond was formed on June 15, 1898, at Garfield School and began a tradition of affiliation with Richmond schools. Ella Bond Johnston was director for 50 years, followed by Louise Whisenhunt for 25 years, and more recently by Marcia Lemon and Ruth Mills-Varnell. An annual art exhibit was held at Garfield on North 8th Street until 1911. In September 1910 three galleries, shown here, were opened at Morton High School, 120 North 9th Street. At present the association's museum is in McGuire Hall at Richmond Senior High School. It was named in honor of Esther McGuire.

Dennis Junior High School at 222 North West 7th Street was named for David Worth Dennis, who taught at Richmond High School from 1875-1879. At Earlham, Dennis taught chemistry from 1873-75 and from 1884-87; he taught biology from 1887-1916.

Joseph Moore School, located on South West 1st Street, was named for Joseph Moore, longtime president of Earlham College. The style shows unusual Flemish/Dutch influence.

Baxter School was built on a farm in West Richmond that had belonged to Robert Morrisson, James Reeves and William Baxter.

Early view of Finley School on the public square between 4th and 5th streets on South B Street. It was named for John Finley, second mayor of Richmond. The ground was donated by John Smith, an early settler.

Sports

The youngsters of Richmond's pioneer families knew only simple games—foot races, tug-of-war battles, throwing balls that actually were rocks covered with buckskin.

With those primitive pleasures in mind, there's little doubt the children and adults of the early 19th Century would find incredible the games—and the facilities for them—played in the late 20th Century in the city they knew as a tiny village.

As the 20th century nears its end, most of the adult and teenage spectator interest is focused on the high school's varsity teams—particularly basketball, football and baseball squads.

That's been true since interscholastic sports competition began in Richmond in the early 1900s, about 100 years after the first settlers came in 1806.

Another longtime sports venue is at nearly 150-year-old Earlham College in Richmond.

But fun and games aren't just for the school and collegiate students. Today, adults—with the leisure time the early settlers also would find incredible—flock to public and private golf courses, bowling centers, softball diamonds, tennis courts, and other areas of athletic competition.

Still, a basketball goal is a magnet for all ages. Youngsters and adults shoot at goals mounted on barns and garages. Churches form leagues. So do industries.

In recent years, a so-called oldtimers' tournament has been staged by Richmond's Eastern Gateway Kiwanis Club. The teams represent the 12 high schools formerly in Wayne County before consolidation trimmed that number to five.

For the last two years, Indiana University East in Richmond has been one of the sites of the nationally known Gus Macker Three-on-Three basketball tournaments.

At the high school, basketball continues to rule as the king—as it does in all of Hoosierdom—in terms of the crowds at 8,000-seat Tiernan Center and in the devotion paid to the annual state high school tournament. The fanaticism climaxed when the high school won its first basketball state championship in 1992.

But the high school's football teams also draw wide support. In fact, the Richmond High School program has won significant state applause as well as mythical state championships in 1956 and 1967. The city has spawned five athletes who played and one who coached in the National Football League.

Furthermore, the Indiana Football Hall of Fame is in Richmond, beckoning visitors to its location in the city's former post office building since 1973.

Baseball, the oldest of the three major sports, also has brought statewide attention to the city. The first major field was Exhibition Park, across from Glen Miller Park and alongside the old National Road (today's U.S. 40). Then came superb Don McBride Stadium (originally Municipal Stadium) built in the early 1930s.

It has been the site of sectional, regional and semi-state competition in the state high school baseball tournament. It's been the home of local American Legion-sponsored teams, composed of high school players, that snared three state championships. And major league exhibition games were played there while it was the home field of a professional Class D team.

Although less visible, high school track and field competition has been a longtime favorite. It is the sport that most closely resembles the games the pioneer youngsters played in clearings cut from the dense forest.

In addition to the state basketball championship won in 1992, the high school golf teams captured state titles in 1941 and 1993 and the wrestling team shared a state championship in 1958.

Other boys varsity sports include cross country, tennis, swimming and soccer.

Girls sports have proliferated in recent decades. The girls varsity teams at RHS include cross country, golf, basketball, gymnastics, swimming, volleyball, softball, tennis, track, and soccer.

At Earlham College, basketball teams coached by Blair Gullion still are remembered by veteran fans. Gullion led the 1931-32 team to a 15-0 season, still the college's only undefeated year in that sport. The string eventually surged to 23 consecutive victories before a loss in the 1932-33 season.

Three decades later, in the early 1960s, the college's football teams grabbed the national spotlight by winning 21 consecutive games, the longest collegiate winning streak in the nation at the time. The string began in the third game of the 1961 season and continued until a 15-2 loss at Kalamazoo in the final game of the 1963 year. The coach: Jerry Huntsman. The quarterback: Rick Carter.

Then, two years later, came the beginning of the college's Camelot years in basketball. Del Harris, later to coach in the NBA, coached Earlham teams to nine consecutive winning seasons (1965-66 through 1973-74).

A Richmond sport little remembered today is roller polo, a game much like ice hockey but with the players competing on roller skates. The 2,500-seat Coliseum frequently sold out for the roller polo games in the early 1900s.

Another team fading from memories is the Richmond Cavaliers, a basketball squad made up largely of Indiana and Ohio college and high school stars. Managed by Robert E. (Bob) Reid, the Cavaliers' triumphs in the late 1920s included three of five exhibition games against teams claiming world titles—two victories over the Cleveland Rosenblums and one over the Brooklyn Visitations.

Arriving on the Richmond sport scene in 1994 is the Richmond Invaders, an amateur football team. Its future, of course, is not known.

But basketball continues to hold a special place in Richmond hearts. And it's true the city can be termed at least one of the cradles of the revered and nationally respected state high school tournament for these reasons:

1. The Indiana High School Athletic Association, governing body of all high school sports in the state, got its start in 1903 during a meeting of Indiana

---

The Gyms of Richmond

Through 1994, Richmond High School has been a sectional tournament host—first level of the four-level state tournament—for 74 years. Richmond was named a sectional site in 1915, first year for the elimination tournament.

Of the 684 games played in the 74 years, 668 were staged on four floors—114 at the Coliseum; 160 at Earlham College's Trueblood Fieldhouse; 334 at Civic Hall; and 60 at Tiernan Center.

Of the remaining 16, one was played at the Richmond YMCA in 1916 due to a heavy schedule at the Coliseum. The other 15 were staged at neighboring Fountain City in 1927 (although RHS was the official host) because of widespread cases of scarlet fever in Richmond.

During the 74 years, 54 schools from eight counties have dispatched teams to Richmond one or more years.

Through 1994, Richmond teams have dominated the sectional, capturing 59 titles and winning 226 games while losing only 15.

The Coliseum

Trueblood Fieldhouse

schools in Richmond.

2. The IHSAA's predecessor organization, the Indiana Interscholastic Athletic Association, was founded in 1899 mainly through the efforts of Richmond High School student Griffith P. Ellis.

3. Several of the early IHSAA leaders were Richmond men, and Arthur L. Trester, an Earlham student, later became the IHSAA commissioner. The prized Trester Award is named for him.

4. Richmond was one of the original 14 sectional sites when those state tournament elimination points were established in 1915. And, Earlham was a regional tournament location in the middle 1920s as was RHS in the late 1980s and early 1990s.

Civic Hall

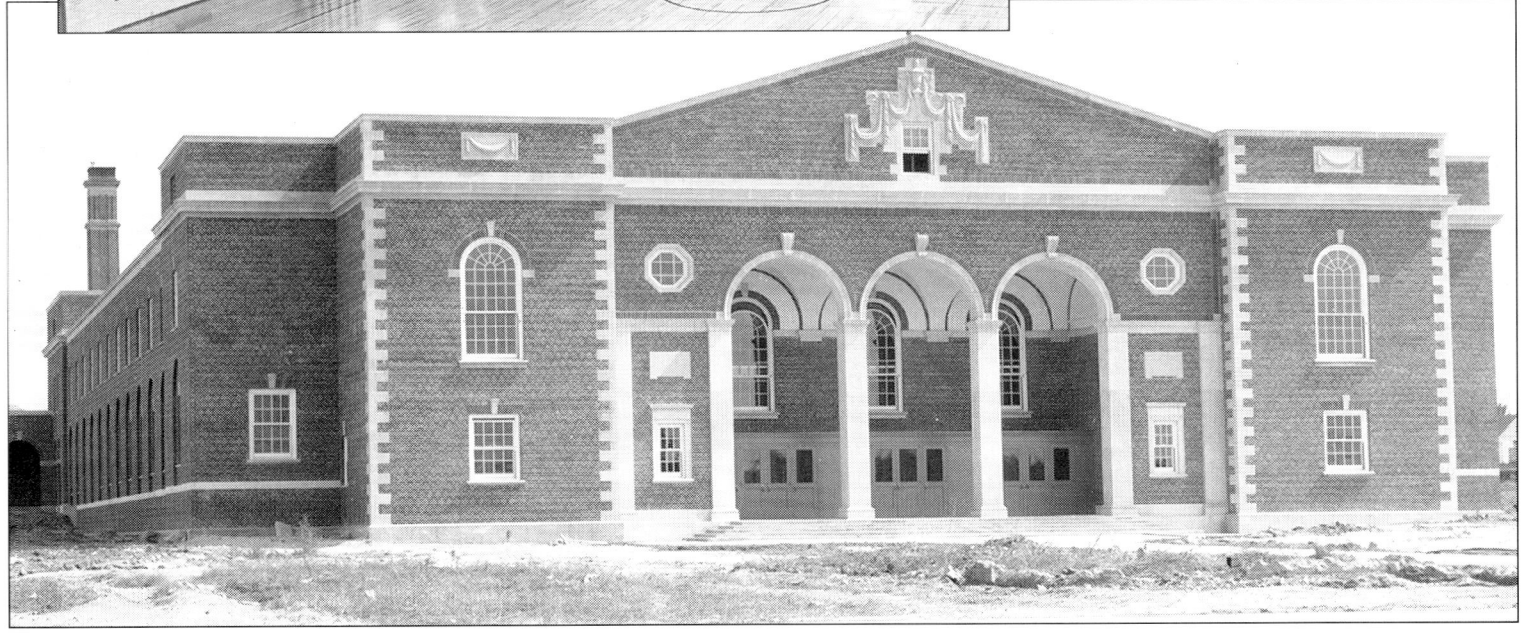

Teiernan Center
The current 8,100-seat facility for RHS is the fourth largest high school gym in the nation.

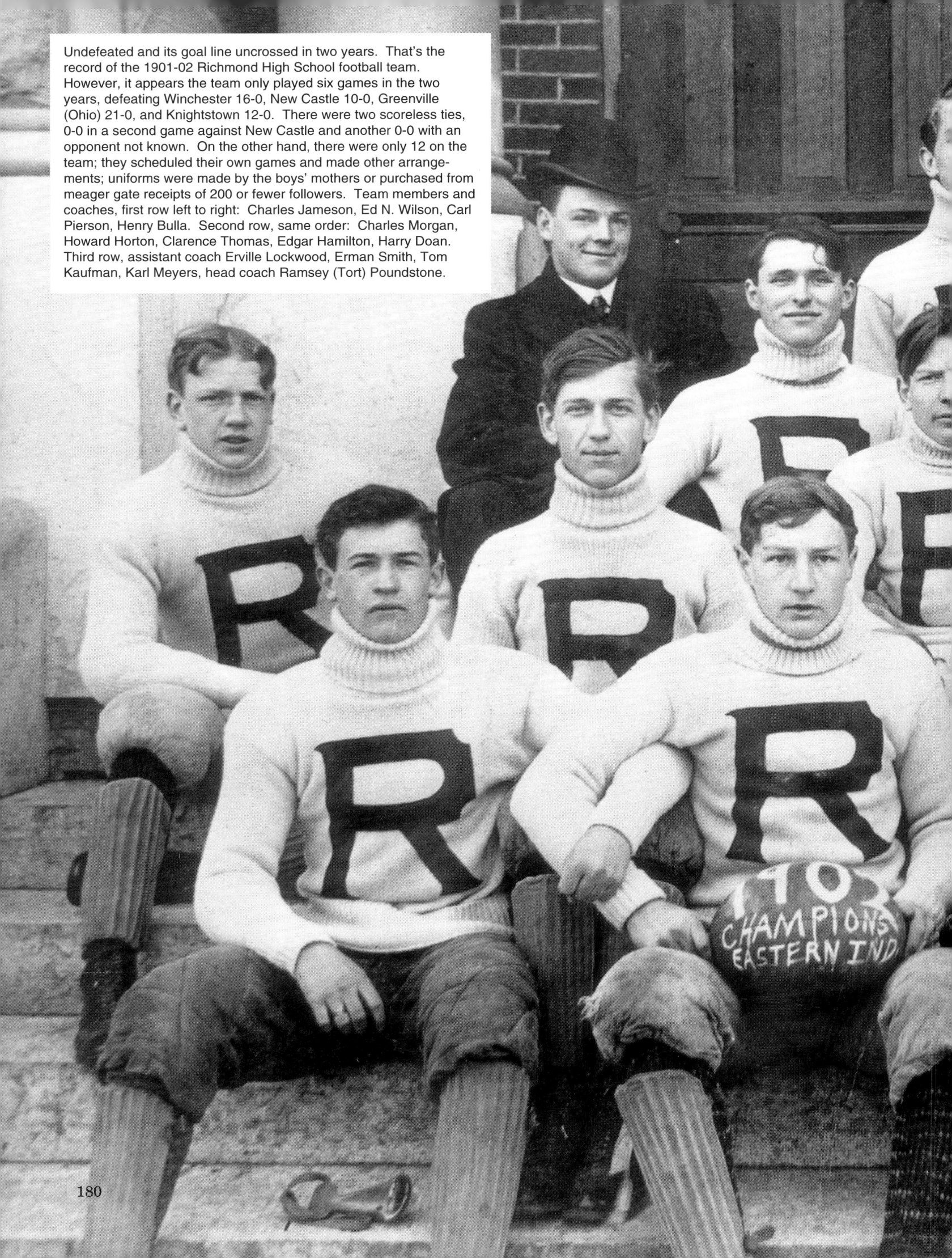

Undefeated and its goal line uncrossed in two years. That's the record of the 1901-02 Richmond High School football team. However, it appears the team only played six games in the two years, defeating Winchester 16-0, New Castle 10-0, Greenville (Ohio) 21-0, and Knightstown 12-0. There were two scoreless ties, 0-0 in a second game against New Castle and another 0-0 with an opponent not known. On the other hand, there were only 12 on the team; they scheduled their own games and made other arrangements; uniforms were made by the boys' mothers or purchased from meager gate receipts of 200 or fewer followers. Team members and coaches, first row left to right: Charles Jameson, Ed N. Wilson, Carl Pierson, Henry Bulla. Second row, same order: Charles Morgan, Howard Horton, Clarence Thomas, Edgar Hamilton, Harry Doan. Third row, assistant coach Erville Lockwood, Erman Smith, Tom Kaufman, Karl Meyers, head coach Ramsey (Tort) Poundstone.

181

Weeb Ewbank

It was a long way from Morton (Richmond) High School to the ranks of professional football coaches, but Richmond native Wilbur (Weeb) Ewbank made it in spades. He's the only coach to lead teams to world championships in both the National Football League (Baltimore Colts in 1958 and 1959) and the American Football League (the New York Jets in 1968).

Ewbank retired as the Jets coach in 1974, then was the team's vice president and general manager before making his home in Oxford, Ohio, home of Miami University.

A 1928 graduate of Miami, often labeled the "cradle of coaches," Ewbank was a three-sport star there—in football, baseball and basketball—just as he was in high school.

In post-college years, he coached Oxford McGuffey High School to unbeaten and unscored-upon seasons. During World War II, he assisted Paul Brown in coaching the Great Lakes Naval Training Station's football squad.

After the war, he led football teams at Washington University in St. Louis and Brown University in Providence, R.I., before rejoining Brown as a member of the Cleveland Browns coaching staff. He became head coach of the Baltimore Colts in 1954. In the years to come, his players included celebrated quarterbacks John Unitas (Colts) and Joe Namath (Jets).

And that's Weeb Ewbank at the microphone, with Joe Namath behind him, as Ewbank presented Namath at a Hall of Fame induction.

That's Weeb Ewbank, third from right in the back row, with his 1922 teammates at Morton High School.

Some of Weeb Ewbank's longtime friends gathered for this photo at a 1959 banquet paying tribute to Ewbank in his home town of Richmond. Left to right: John Rizio, Gabe Kennedy, Ather Reeg, Ewbank, Bob Reid (rear), Weeb's father Charles Ewbank, Miami University trainer Jay Colville, and Miami U. athletic director John Brickles.

Professional football's Tim Brown spent early years in Richmond but was graduated from Knightstown Morton Memorial High School. After graduation from Ball State University, he was drafted by the Green Bay Packers in 1959, but was released shortly. He eventually played nine full seasons with the Philadelphia Eagles. In 1962, his 2,300 yards running, pass receiving and kick returning broke an NFL mark—and he surpassed that total by more than 1,000 yards in 1963. He ended his pro career with the Baltimore Colts in 1968 and 1969.

James Z. Logan, retired Richmond surgeon, is believed to be Richmond"s first professional football player. He was a guard one year with the Chicago Bears, and a member of the 1943 team that defeated the Washington Redskins 41-21 for the NFL title. Logan, 1935 Morton (Richmond) High School graduate, was a high school quarterback but a guard at Indiana University where he captained the team in 1939. He was a member of the college all-star team pitted in 1940 against the professional Green Bay Packers in an annual college-pro game.

Running back Vagas Ferguson was all-state at RIchmond High School and an all-American at the University of Notre Dame. His 3,472 yards gained (1976-79) is second best in the Irish's storied history. Drafted by the New England Patriots, he established a Patriot rookie rushing record with 818 yards on 211 carries in 1980. An injured ankle jolted his pro career in 1981 and 1982. He later was signed but played little with the NFL's Houston, Cleveland and Tampa Bay teams. He became Richmond High School's athletic director in the early 1990s.

Hubert (Hub) Etchison, legendary Richmond High School football coach, led his teams to a 180-63-7 record in 25 years (1953 through 1977). The quarter century included three undefeated teams—9-0 in 1956 and a mythical state championship; 9-0 in 1958; 10-0 in 1967 and another mythical state title; 10 outright North Central Conference titles plus one shared.

Football receiver Paul Flatley was all-state at Richmond High School in 1959 and an all-American at Northwestern University. He was the NFL rookie of the year in 1963 while playing for the MInnesota Vikings, and was a member of the Pro Bowl team in 1967 while a member of the Atlanta Falcons.

Offensive end Lamar Lundy was all-state at Richmond High School in 1952 and an all-American at Purdue University where he was the university's first-ever most valuable player in both football and basketball. As a defensive end he played 13 years for the professional Los Angeles Rams where he was a member of the famed Fearsome Foursome.

Trester Winners

Indiana basketball's prestigious Trester (previously Gimbel) Award has been won by three Richmond High School players—Phillip Kessler in 1924, James (Sammy) Lyboult in 1935 and Todd Graf in 1985.

**James Lyboult
1935**

Phillip Kessler - 1924

Todd Graf - 1985

Elder Eberhart's Richmond High School basketball teams posted a 203-126 record in his 13 years as head coach (1932-33 through 1944-45). His 1934-35 squard was the first RHS team to reach the Final Four of the state tournament. His sectional tournament record in games won was a glossy 43-2, and included 11 championships. His teams also won three regional tournaments.

Richard E. (Dick) Baumgartner is the winningest coach in RHS basketball history (through 1994). In 12 years (1965-66 through 1976-77), his record was 234-73. His teams were unblemished at the sectional level, 33-0 in games and 12 championships. He also snared eight regional titles (1966,1968, 1969, 1972, 1973, 1974, 1976, 1977), breaking rival Muncie's usual grasp at that level of the state tournament.

George Griffith coached RHS to its first state basketball championship in 1992. His team defeated Lafayette Jefferson 77-73 in overtime in the title game after tripping Jeffersonville 94-92, also in overtime. His record at RHS was 214-74 and included nine sectional, six regional and three semistate titles in 11 years (1982-83 through 1992-93). His teams surged to the state tournament's final game in two other years, losing to Marion both trips, 74-67 in 1985 and 69-56 in 1987.

Del Harris, who will coach the National Basketball Association's Los Angles Lakers in the 1994-95 season, never had a losing year at Earlham College in Richmond. In nine years coaching basketball at the college (1965-66 through 1973-74), his record was 175-70. His previous coaching experience in the NBA: 1979-80 through 1982-83 at Houston and 1987-88 through 1991-92 at Milwaukee.

Richmond High School's Charles (Woody) Austin was Indiana's Mr. Basketball in 1988, the first RHS player to capture the state honor. As of 1994, he was by far the school's career leader in points scored with 1,900 in four years (the school years of 1984-85 through 1987-88). He holds school scoring records in several other categories. He played his collegiate years at Purdue University.

Kara and Jody Griffith, daughters of Coach George Griffith, and Chris Bailey, the coach's son-in-law, pose with the first sign erected after the team won the championship. The sign is near the city's Municipal Building.

1992 Champions

Jubilant Richmond High School basketball team members and coaches celebrate moments after they won the 1992 state basketball championship. Team members: Jackie Bledsoe, Billy Wright, Chad Austin, Alan Rule, Brent Hampton, Robert Sanders, Dedric Thompson, Jerrad Powers, Rob Sinkan, Chris Warfel, Gref Lynch, Damon Lewis. Head coach: George Griffith. Assistant coach: Jeff Williams. Principal: R. Dennis Renshaw. Athletic director: Vagas Ferguson.

In pre-radio years (let alone television), Richmond's avid baseball fans followed the progress of World Series games via electrically operated scoreboards set up by both Richmond newpapers, the *Palladium* and the *Item*. (See crowd photo). Then from 1922-34, the *Palladium's* scoreboard featured a magnetic ball manipulated from behind the board to track the games' developments. Richmond's only known major league players: Claude Berry and Glenn S. (Pete) Chapman. Berry played with the Chicago White Sox, the Philadelphia Athletics and Pittsburgh in the Federal League in the early 1900s. Chapman played with the Brooklyn Dodgers in 1934-35.

Don McBride

This photo was taken in the summer of 1994 as preparations began for a game at McBride Stadium (formerly Municipal Stadium). Built in the early 1930s, the stadium was renamed in 1984 as a tribute to Don McBride's 29 years as superintendent of Richmond parks. The stadium has been the site of high school sectional, regional and semistate tournaments and American Legion team tournament. It was also the home of Class D professional teams in post-World War II years.

Champions of Richmond

Records kept by the *Richmond Palladium-Item*, the city's daily newspaper, show the following individual state champions (plus a relay team) through the years at Richmond High School.

TRACK
Ralph Guyer, hammer throw, 1905.
Karl Allison, high hurdles and low hurdles, 1909.
Everett Veregge, high hurdles and low hurdles, 1946.
Bill Satterfield, 100-yard dash and 220-yard dash, 1956.
Bill Satterfield, 220-yard dash, 1957.
Mike Leavell, Price Faulkner, Don Williams and Terry Hogg, mile relay, 1964
John Henderson, 440-yard dash, 1972 and 1973.
Marion Burns, 100-yard dash and 220-yard dash, 1973.
Roger Frazier, 100-yard dash, 1975.
Jeff Campbell, 800-meter run, 1982.
Nathan Davis, shot put, 1991 and 1992.

BASKETBALL
Richmond High School players named Indiana basketball all-stars and the years they were selected:
Mack Payton, 1942.
Ralph Holmes, 1943.
Dave Bruck, 1946.
Lamar Lundy, 1953.
Rick Risinger, 1969.
Rick Thalls, 1972.
Rob Willis, 1977.
Todd Graf, 1985.
Jerry Coleman, 1987.
Woody Austin, 1988 (Mr. Basketball).
Stacie Sheperd, 1990 (runnerup for Miss Basketball).
Billy Wright, 1992.
Chad Austin, 1993.
Jerrad Powers, 1994.

WRESTLING
David Rader, 95 pounds, 1958.
Gary Murr, 133 pounds, 1959.
Paul Lewis, 138 pounds, 1959.
Jeff Virgne, 133 pounds, 1961.
Mike King, 126 pounds, 1972.

OTHERS
Val Young, all-around gymnastics and vaulting, 1976.
Cathy Crum, girls' golf, 1978.
Chris Coveney, boys' 100-meter breaststroke, 1981.
Shelly Stoner, girls' intermediate vaulting, 1981.

The Richmond High School wrestling team shared a state championship with Broad Ripple High School of Indianapolis in 1958. Team members and coaches are, front row, left to right: Gary Murr, Dave Rader, Jerry Zucker, Jim Sticco. Second row: Jack Myers, Ken Jordan, Nick Kovach, manager Matt Mercurio. Third row: coach Charles Hilton, Link Lewis, Ken York, Alvin Johnson, Paul Lewis, assistant coach Ray Amigo. Team member Wayne Watkins was not present for the photo.

This American Legion-sponsored baseball team won a state championship in 1939, defeating Jasper 2-1 at Richmond Municipal Stadium (now McBride Stadium). The bat boy in front is Barney Runnels. First row, left to right: Gene Harvey, Bob O'Maley, Skip Runnels, Gene Curry, Jack O'Maley, Delbert Duckworth, Billy Hart, Seldon (Red) Albano. Second row: coach Lawrence Maplesden, Paul Marksbury, Zeke Stolle, Mack Peyton, James Cox, Clay Memze, Bill Kaeuper, Harry Davidson, and Legion member Z. Jay Stanley. Other Richmond Legion teams captured state championships in 1947 and 1958.

Richmond High School's 1941 golf team won the school's first-ever state team championship in any sport. With a score of 322, the team bested a field of 49 other school squads at the Speedway course in Indianapolis. Team members are, left to right: John Juhasz, Leo Bruck, John Suveges, Mike Portanova. Kneeling is the coach, Charles McNaughton.

RHS's 1993 golf team brought the school its latest state championship (as of the fall of 1994) with a two-day total of 618 at the Golf Club of Prestwick in Avon. Team members and others are, front row left to right: J. J. Cornett, Bo Van Pelt, Ryan Cate. Back row: school principal John Lebo, assistant coach Paul Bechtold, Chad Witherby, Greg Givens, Ron Melling, coach Joe Moehring, and athletic director Vagas Ferguson.

Historic Houses of Richmond

Buildings are visible and tangible reminders of our past. They remind us of the architects, the builders and those who invested their time, talent and funds in the city.

Richmond is fortunate to have an array of homes that represent 175 years of history. The earliest include the log houses of Solomon Dickinson and Nathan Hawkins standing at the Wayne County Historical Museum. There are at least two log buildings under protective siding on South 6th Street.

The Federal period is shown in the four-bay brick John Eggemeyer house at 400 South 4th Street and the Hall house at 119 South 3rd Street.

Several outstanding examples of Greek Revival style should be mentioned. Two types survive. One is the modest one and one-half story cottage with the usual gable end toward the street. Good examples are the Raukopf cottage at 405 South E Street and the house at 117 South 5th Street.

The other Greek Revival style is the massive, usually square, two-story home with a cupola or belvedere. The Coffin house at 102 South 3rd Street exemplifies this style. Another is the Laws house at 104 Fort Wayne Avenue. The Evans home in Spring Grove was this type, but has been modified. Also of note is the Maxwell house, 228 College Avenue, now part of Earlham College's School of Religion.

The Italianate and Italian Villa styles were popular during much of Richmond's commercial expansion and many Main Street buildings show the Italian influence, usually distinguished by brackets supporting the eaves. In the Starr Historic District some earlier styles were brought up to date by the addition of Italianate features. In general, verticality was emphasized with tall windows in a narrow building and a low-pitch hip roof. Often the windows were topped with decorative caps, usually formed of tin.

The French Second Empire style shows well in a brick dwelling at 100 South 13th Street. A mansard roof is typical and created a large space for attic storage. The Abram Gaar Mansion, 2593 Pleasant View Road, is in this style and has been gracefully restored.

The Romanesque Revival style was better suited to large civic or commercial buildings, but the Sudhoff house at 228 South 4th Street is a fine example. The Edward Eggemeyer house, 234

Solomon Dickinson's two-story log house was moved from Fort Wayne Avenue to the grounds of the Wayne County Historical Museum. Dickinson opened a tinsmith shop in 1821 on Main Street between Fifth and Sixth streets.

Lefevre Cranstone, an English artist, came to the United States to visit relatives and stayed in Richmond in 1858-60. His watercolors of local scenes are excellent records of those years. They are owned by Indiana University and the Boston Museum of Art. His relative in Richmond, William Lefevre, lived on North 10th Street. In the distance is the Noah Leeds home, now the site of the former Atlas Underwear Company. The adjacent residence was built by Charles Henry, then the next one by Job Brown. North C Street crosses at this point and then there are two double townhouses, still standing.

South 4th, has some features of this style, but tends toward Queen Anne.

The Queen Anne homes seem to be a collection of parts formed into an imposing mass, often with columned porches, turrets, stained glass windows, supplemental gables and more than one exterior covering. Window glass was easily obtained so windows were often large. The Stratton house at 203 North 15th Street exemplifies these features.

At the turn of the century Colonial Revival took center stage and many homeowners added decorative touches such as classically columned porches and gables with cartouches. A number of Colonial Revival and Georgian homes were constructed in the Reeveston neighborhood.

The west side of the city is especially rich in examples of the Bungalow style, usually a one or one-and-one-half story home with a gable end to the street.

Americus Pogue of Pogue, Miller & Company lived in this French Second Empire style home at 1416 East Main Street. It was designed by Stephen O. Yates (1854-1924), Richmond architect. The carriage house at right belonged to the Jonas Gaar family; Jonas was married to Fanny Pogue, daughter of Americus.

Jonas Gaar's home at 1426 East Main Street still stands. However, it is considerably altered, and there is a small business building occupying the front yard. Two apartment buildings on North 15th Street were commissioned by Jonas Gaar, an officer in Pogue, Miller & Company, a retail hardware business.

Left: The John M. Gaar family appears on the decorative porch of their home at 26 North 8th Street. Left to right are: Mrs. Matthew Rattray, mother of both the first and second wives of John; Helen R. Gaar (second wife), John Milton Gaar, Jeanette Gaar (later Leeds), William who married Julia Meek, and John Milton, Jr., who died as a youth.

The Burton Carr house at the northeast corner of South 15th and A streets was on the site of Sycamore Square apartments. The house was built of round, water-washed stones.

High Tower House, 326 North 10th Street, was erected by the Starr family for James Starr as a simple Federal-style home. There has been extensive remodeling. Later owners included Henry D. Chapin and Charles and Gertie Kolp. The Kolps taught dancing and were sometimes on the road with their vaudeville act. They often entertained theatrical performers who came to Richmond on tour. In 1994 the residence is owned and has been restored by a member of the Stegall-Berheide-Orr Funeral Home.

Dr. T. Henry Davis' house, 1021 Main Street, is in the French Second Empire style. It displays in this instance a concave Mansard roof on the main section and a convex curve on the tower roof. The home was torn down circa 1979.

Dr. T. Henry Davis (1836-1932), born on Nantucket Island, practiced medicine until he was 90 years old. He advocated a city water works as an important health measure and he contributed several whale vertebrae to the Joseph Moore Museum at Earlham.

The Raukopf cottage, 405 South E Street, is a typical Greek Revival home, a style popular with many German immigrants.

This handsome Italianate house with cupola was built c. 1858 for Andrew Finley Scott (1811-1895) and family. He became one of the founders and the president of Second National Bank, now Star Bank. The Scott family was in residence here until 1973 when the home was given to the Wayne County Historical Museum. It is open by appointment.

Col. John Miller's home on Chester Pike was later used by Reid Memorial Hospital as a residence for nurses. Cut stone is the building medium used in this eclectic style house.

The William Baxter home at 321 Lincoln Street in West Richmond was originally the elegant brick house built by Robert Morrisson. It was purchased by James Reeves and remodeled, then sold to Baxter, an Englishman who turned the property into a model farm. When the farm was subdivided the rear wing of the house was demolished and the back of the house became the front when Lincoln Street was laid out.

This imposing structure at 510 West Main Street was for many years the home of the Thomas Harrison family. Harrison graduated from Earlham College in 1880, studied architecture and designed several of the college buildings before moving to Indianapolis. He designed a pulley system to open a roof vent, allowing warm air to leave the house in summer. The home was demolished by Interfaith Apartments.

David Sutton, formerly of Milton, built his Italian Villa at 1503 National Road West in 1875 when he and L. L. Lawrence brought the Wayne Agricultural Works to Richmond. At present it is in danger of being razed.

Richmond Today

After the explosions and fires of April 6, 1968, several blocks of Main Street were converted to a pedestrian promenade with fountains, benches, trees, shrubs, flowers, and mushroom-shaped structures to provide shade.

Indiana University East grew out of the Earlham College-Indiana University Education Center of 1946. Its aim was to serve an adult population whose schedules prevented them from attending daytime classes. A fund-raising campaign was initiated in the fall of 1969 and a site for a community college was selected on U.S. 27 near I-70. The main building on campus is Whitewater Hall. Other buildings include Brice Hayes Hall and a solar greenhouse.

Left: Thanks to the vision and hard work of Joe Longstreth, Sandy Lingle and the Civic Hall Associates, the Richmond Senior High School gymnasium has been transformed into a spacious Performing Arts Center. The group's campaign raised funds to create an auditorium, stage, rehearsal rooms and reception area. The facility is home to the Richmond Symphony Orchestra and hosts a number of productions.

Hill's Pet Nutrition, Inc., opened its plant at 2325 Union Pike in 1991 to manufacture Science Diet and Prescription Diet brand pet foods. In 1994 the company received the prestigious U.S. Senate Productivity award, one of 50 nationwide and the only one awarded in Indiana. An expansion is planned in the near future. Marc Swartz is Facility Director.

The Courthouse Annex houses administrative offices of Wayne County. Designed by George Clinton, Richmond architect, the annex was intended to enhance the view of the 1893 courthouse, not interfere with it. Its sunken position saves on heating and cooling costs and the abundant windows allow views of the sky above.

Acknowledgements

The author extends her sincere thanks to a great many individuals who helped to bring this pictorial history of Richmond to completion. The Advisory Committee has been of major importance by bringing their knowledge and enthusiasm to the task. We discussed topics, selected photographs, wrote captions and sections and provided conversation, inspiration and glasses of iced tea as needed.

I am grateful to the helpful persons who entrusted their photographs, books and pamphlets to us, and to Trudy Hobbs of Star Bank who received them, to Star Bank which provided financial support for the project and permitted Trudy Hobbs to assist us.

We could not have produced the book without the opportunity to examine the photographic files of the *Palladium-Item* newspaper. These files have been essential to the success of the book. Emmett Smelser, publisher of the newspaper, has been supportive of the project and we are most appreciative. Helen Williamson, *Palladium-Item* librarian, has been unfailingly patient and cheerful in spite of our interruption of her daily schedule. We are grateful for use of space for meetings and discussions at the Neighborhood Clearinghouse and the Design Center on Main Street.

At the Wayne County Historical Museum, Michele Bottorff and her staff were gracious and helpful whenever we needed their assistance. The staff of the Reference Department at Morrisson-Reeves Library was always responsive to our frequent requests for microfilms.

David Marsee, local artist, has provided an excellent view of Richmond from the west bank of the Whitewater Gorge on the colorful dust jacket. Dr. George Blakey, assistant professor of history at Indiana University East, has my gratitude for taking time from his teaching duties to examine the proof sheets and write the foreword. This enterprise was begun with the vision, focus and perseverance of Brad Baraks and his talented staff. Without them the book would have remained a mirage. We trust that it will please its readers and foster an appreciation of Richmond by her citizens.

Advisory Committee

Photos by Bill Wallace

Helen Williamson
Palladium-Item
Librarian

Standing (l to r):
Dick Reynolds
James P. Hartig
Seated:
Myra J. Coate
Gertrude Ward
(author)
Jean Prichard

Bibliography

Anonymous. 1899. *Biographical and Genealogical History of Wayne, Fayette, Union and Franklin Counties.* Lewis Publishing Co. Chicago.

Beisner, L.R. 1979. *A Time before Us.* Illustrated by E. Loar. Beisner and Loar, [Richmond, Indiana.]

Blockson, C.L. 1987. *The Underground Railroad.* Prentice Hall Press, New York.

Dalbey's [E. and W.]. 1896. *Pictorial History of the City of Richmond.* Nicholson Printing and Manufacturing Company, Richmond, Indiana.

Dalbey's [E. and W.] 1906. *Pictorial History of the City of Richmond.* Nicholson Printing and Manufacturing Company, Richmond, Indiana.

Emswiler, G.P. 1897. Poems and Sketches. Nicholson Printing and Manufacturing Company, Richmond, Indiana.

Feeger, L.M. [1973.] *A Brief History of Early Richmond.* Wayne County Historical Society, Richmond, Indiana.

Fox, H.C. 1912. *Memoirs of Wayne County and the City of Richmond, Indiana.* Vols. I, II. (repr.) Unigraphic, Inc., Evansville, Indiana.

Goodwell, M.E. 1987. First Presbyterian Church, Richmond, Indiana, 1837-1987. Graphic Press, Inc., Richmond, Indiana.

Hartig, J.P. and G.L. Ward. 1991. Gaar Houses, Richmond, Indiana. Neighborhood Preservation Services, Inc., Centerville, Indiana.

Hamm, T.D. 1988. *The Transformation of American Quakerism, Orthodox Friends, 1800-1907.* Indiana University Press, Bloomington.

Kennedy, R. 1994. *Jelly Roll, Bix, and Hoagy.* Indiana University Press, Bloomington.

Knollenberg, B. 1945. *Pioneer Sketches of the Upper Whitewater Valley.* Indiana Historical Society, Indianapolis.

[Lemon, M.] 1978. Art in Richmond, 1898-1978. Art Association of Richmond. Paul Graphics, Inc. [Richmond, Indiana]

:Lockridge, R. F. 1953. *The Story of Indiana.* Harlow Publishing Corporation, Oklahoma City, Oklahoma.

Miller, W. 1982. Indiana Newspaper Bibliography. Indiana Historical Society, Indianapolis.

Plummer, J. T. A Directory to the City of Richmond. R.O. Dormer & W.R. Holloway, [Richmond, Indiana].

Rafinesque, C.S. 1954. *Walum Olum or Red Score.* Indiana Historical Society, Indianapolis.

Royer, D. M. 1993. The German-American Contribution to Richmond's Development. Royer Augustin Printers. Richmond, Indiana.

Thornburgh, O. 1963. *Earlham, the Story of the College, 1847-1962.* The Earlham College Press, Richmond, Indiana.

Walters, B. L. 1972. *Furniture Makers of Indiana*, 1793 to 1850. Indiana Historical Society, Indianapolis.

[Wasson, J.M.] 1875. *Annals of Pioneer Settlers of the Whitewater and its Tributaries from 1804 to 1830.* Telegram Printing Company, Richmond.

Wissler, W. O. 1912. The Mills of Wayne County, Indiana. (Manuscript prepared for Earlham College.)

Young, A.W. 1872. *History of Wayne County, Indiana.* Robert Clark and Company, Cincinnati.

[Young, A.W.] 1884. *History of Wayne County.* Vols. I, II. Inter-State Publishing Company, Chicago.

Yount, B. W. 1969. Tombstone Inscriptions in Wayne County, Indiana. Vols. 1-4. Fort Wayne Public Library, Fort Wayne, Indiana.

Contributors

Seldon Albano
Charles Austin
Roland Batchelor
Philip Birck & Son, Inc.
Martha Bradshaw
Jan Clark
Myra J. Coate
Randy and Cathy Crowe
Marjorie Duning
Howard G. Duke
Earlham College
Weeb Ewbank
Don Fasnacht
Vagas Ferguson
Paul Flatley
Fosters' Antique Gallery
Joyce Graf
George Griffith
Thomas D. Hamm
Mary Harding
Hill's Pet Nutrition, Inc.
David A. Hogg
J.M. Hutton Co., Inc.
Indiana Football Hall of Fame
John Juhasz
Don and Janice Kahle
Esther C. Kellner
Robert Kenworthy
Charles Kienzle
Mazine Klein
Kramer & Associates
Mildred LaFuze
Harry Leavell
Marcia Lemon
James Z. Logan
David Marsee
Don McBride
Phyllis McGairk
Janet Misner
William and Mary Ellen Misner
Peg Moore
Tana Moore
Palladium-Item
Harold K. Petry
Ralph Pyle, Jr.
Richmond Art Museum
Dick Reynolds
Kevin Risch
Charles Smelser
Francis T. Stanley
Star Bank
Bob Van Pelt
Wayne County Historical Museum
Wayne Dairy Products, Inc.
Francis Woolworth

Index

A
Abington, 21, 31
Adena, 10
American Football League, 182
American Red Cross, 153
Art Association of Richmond, 98-99, 175
Atlas Underwear Co., 55, 190
Autohaus, 139
Automobiles, 36-37, 52
Autrey, Gene, 119

B
Banks, 16, 29, 63, 84-87, 97, 116, 193
Bartel, Adam H., 24, 54
Baseball, 189
Basketball, 186, 188
Baxter, William, 176, 194
Bates, Nathaniel, 131
Belle Vue Place, 170
Birck, Philip & Son, Inc. 57, 60
Bicycles, 91-92
Bridges, 21, 144, 148
Bryan, William Jennings, 119, 124
Buhl, Christian, 20

C
Cascade Nursery, 114
Casket business, 48
Cathell, Edna Stubbs, 98, 151
Centerville, 16, 94, 98, 128
Chase Piano Co., 50, 118
Chautauqua, 108
Churches, 99, 117, 118, 132, 152, 158-165
City Building, 21, 135-136, 138, 140-142
City Market, 67
Civic Hall, 178-179, 195
Civil War, 6, 28, 101, 119, 129, 132
Coliseum, 137, 178
Coffin, Levi, 94, 127
Commercial Club, 42, 44, 64, 108
Costigan, Francis, 116
Cox, Jeremiah, Jr., 17
Cox, Jeremiah, Sr., 16, 17, 27, 150

D
D.A.R., 15, 17
Dennis, David W., 109, 169
Dickinson, Charles, 118, 123
Dille & McGuire Co., 53

E
Earlham Cemetery, 105, 149
Earlham College, 12, 62, 94, 96, 98, 101, 106-107, 109, 114, 151, 166, 174, 176-177, 179
Eggemeyer, John M., 70, 190
Elder-Beerman, 145
Eubank, Wilbur (Weeb, 182
Explosion of 1968, 111, 145

F
F & N Lawn Mowers, 16, 53
Fallen Timbers, Battle of, 14-15
Feeger, Luther M., 13, 99, 102
Fire Chiefs, 135
Fire Department, 133-136
Football Team, R.H.S., 180-181
Foulke, William Dudley, 17, 102, 106
Fountain City, 54, 127, 178

Fox, Judge Henry Clay, 98
French, Jesse, Piano and Organ Co., 119

G
Gaar, A. & Co., 41, 43
Gaar, Abram, 40, 42, 94, 190
Gaar, John Milton, 16, 40, 42, 53, 116, 191
Gaar, Jonas, 40, 42, 191
Gaar, Julia Meek, 94, 191
Gaar, Scott & Co., 16, 23, 41-43, 53, 146
Gennett, Clarence, 119, 124
Gennett, Henry, 50, 119
Gennett Records, 119, 124
Glen Miller Park, 17, 32, 37, 64, 91, 93, 104, 106, 108-109, 154, 177
Golf teams, R. H. S., 189
Greenville Treaty, 11, 14-15, 128

H
Hagerstown, 13, 19, 94-95, 131
Harris, Del, 177, 185
Hasecoster, John, 43, 58, 71, 84, 136, 139-140, 150, 152
Hayes Regional Arboretum, 89, 94, 106
Hayes, Stanley, W., 106
Henley, Micajah, 37, 90, 93
Hill, E. G., 97-98, 114
Hill, Joseph, 61
Hill, Sarah, 97
Hill's Pet Nutrition, Inc., 195
Holloway, David, 16
Home Telephone Co., 143
Hoosier Drill Co., 64
Hoosier's Nest, 16, 18, 142
Hoover, David, 11-12, 16-17, 22
Hoover, George, 94, 128-129
Hoover, Herbert, 109
Hospitals, 13, 26, 152, 193
Hotels, 24, 35, 48, 63-66, 81
Hutton, J. M. & Co., 49

I
Indiana Football Hall of Fame, 94, 147, 177
Indiana University East, 177, 195
International Harvester Co., 39, 45
Interurban 23, 34
Item newspaper, 57, 187

J
Jazz, 125
Jenkins, C. Francis, 101
Jenkinson, Isaac, 102
Johnston, Ella Bond, 99, 175
Jones, Isaac, 40
Jones, Thomas E. 169
Jordan, Dulcinea Masob, 101

K
Kahle Brothers, 71
Kelly-Hutchinson Building, 33, 57, 60, 84, 87, 114
Kessler, Phillip, 184
Kielhorn, Mrs. Augustus, 77
Klein, George, 63
Knights of Pythias, 117, 160
Knollenberg, George H., 54, 58
Knollenberg's Store, 57-59, 115
Kolp, Elizabeth, 123

L
Lawnmowers, 53
Leeds, Jeanette Gaar, 102, 191
Leeds, Rudolph G., 96-97, 102-103
Library, 150
Liederkranz Society, 118
Light Plant, 146
Longstreth, Joe, 125, 195

M
Madonna of the Trail, 17
Mayors, 126
McGuire Hall, 94, 99, 175
Miller, Col. John, 152, 193
Mills, 13, 23, 55
Moore, Joseph, 94, 169, 176
Morrisson, Robert, 60, 76, 84, 150, 176
Morrisson-Reeves Library, 150
Mote, Marcus, 16, 100
Museums, 94

N
Namath, Joe, 182
National Football League, 182
National Road, 11, 14, 20-21, 27, 34, 94, 98, 128, 149, 177
Nicholson Printing and Manufacturing Co., 162
Nicholson, Timothy, 62
Nixon Paper Mill, 23
North Carolina, 11
Northwest Ordinances, 11
Northwest Territory, 11, 14

O
Observatory, 166
Odd Fellows Whitewater Lodge Orchestra, 120-121
Ordovician Period, 18, 27
Osnabrueck, 71

P
Palladium, 16, 18, 52, 102, 142, 187
Palladium-Item, 13, 16, 99, 103
Palladium Publishing Co., 102-103
Parks, 104-108, 155-177
Pianos, 118
Police Chiefs, 132
Popp, John, 118, 123
Price's Confectionery, 83
Promenade, 113, 145, 195
Prophetstown, 15

Q
Quaker Trace, 81
Quinn, Rev. William Paul, 160
Quigley's Drugstore, 81

R
Railroads, 22-23, 97, 148
Reid, Daniel G., 16, 53-54, 85, 97, 117, 152, 161
Revolutionary War, 10, 16
Richmond Art Museum, 94
Richmond Baking Co., 23, 30, 43
Richmond-Brookville Canal, 13, 19
Richmond Civic Theater, 110
Richmond Motorcycle Club, 89
Richmond Natural Gas Co., 16
Richmond Nursery, 114
Richmond Symphony Orchestra, 195

Richmond Water Works, 143
Rose Hill Milk, 61
Roses, 97-98

S
Salisbury, 15, 31, 62, 128
Schools, 96, 123, 149, 156, 172-178, 182-183
Scott, Andrew Finley, 85-86, 193
Smith, John, 11, 16-17, 60, 141-142, 176
Spanish-American War, 154
Starr, James M., 118-119, 144, 192
Starr Piano Co., 23, 38, 50, 119, 124
Streetcars, 29, 32-33
Sun-Telegram, 108
Sutton, David, 31, 194
Swayne, Robinson & Co., 46-47, 82, 119

T
Tallyho, 29
Teas, Edward Y., 114
Tecumseh, 14, 15, 141
Thomas, Dr. Mary, 101
Threshing, 44
Tiernan Center, 177-179
Townsend Community Center, 127, 153
Townsend, James M., 127
Truman, Harry S, 17

U
Underground Railroad, 94, 127
Union Station, 24
Unitas, John, 182

V
Vigrans Variety Store, 145
Vincennes, 15

W
Warner, Building, 22
Warner, Dr. Ithamar, 22, 140
Wayne Agricultural Co., 31, 37, 52, 194
Wayne County Courthouse, 21, 128; annex, 195
Wayne County Historical Museum, 94-95, 131, 171, 190, 193
Wayne Dairy Products Co., 61
Wayne, Gen. Anthony, 14-15
Wernle Orphans' Home, 170
Whitewater Gorge, 10, 21-22, 148
Whitewater River, 11, 13, 20, 23, 27, 40, 78, 82, 143, 146
Whitewater Valley, 19, 50, 118-119
Williams, Gaar, 96
World War I, 13, 115
World War II, 55, 125
Wrestling Champions, 188
Wrigley, Sarah Finley, 151

Y
Yates, Stephen O., 63, 119
Y. M. C. A., 178
Young, Andrew, 99

Z
Zimmerman, Dr. William W., 37, 126, 142

An 1859 sketch of Richmond, Indiana.

The warm ambiance of the Elks City Club in 1937.

Star Bank

Presidents

Andrew Scott
1872-1895
William Scott
1895-1897
John Gaar
1897-1900
John Dougan
1900-1914
Samual Gaar
1914-1929
Albert Mathews
1930-1932
Dudley Elmer
1933-1952
Ernest Elleman
1953-1958
Benjamin Johnson
July-1958-Dec.1958
Jesse Parshall
1959-1962
F. Wayne Stidham
1962-1974
William King
1974-1982
Kenneth Bane
1982-1994
Gregory W. Edwards
April- 1994- June-1994
(promoted to Chairman/CEO)
David W. Stidham
June-1994 to present

The author, advisors, and publisher would like to thank Star Bank for its efforts to preserve and record Richmond history through sponsorship of Richmond: A Pictorial History. *Preservation is progress, too.*

The lobby of Star Bank's main facility in Richmond at Promenade and 8th streets before it was remodeled.

The East Main Street Branch of Star Bank on the old National Road.